THE GREENING

OF

WILD PLACES

Patrick Goodland

D1232167

English village life over two centuries –
The story of Gorsley Baptist Church
1800 – 2002

First published 2002

ISBN 0-9542928-0-4

Set in Baskerville.
Printed in Great Britain by Print Plus,
Hereford, HR4 9HN.

Cover water-colour picture by
Jim Shakespeare.

Further copies of this book are available from the
Gorsley Baptist Church, Gorsley, Ross-on-Wye,
Herefordshire. HR9 7SE.
Telephone/Fax: 01989 720312
e-mail: admin@gorsleychapel.co.uk

CONTENTS

FOREWORD

I well remember my first visit to Gorsley Baptist church. I was warned it would be like travelling to the middle of nowhere only to discover you were at the centre of the universe.

This may seem an extravagant claim for a Herefordshire village, but Gorsley has served as a unique gathering place for thousands of Christians from all parts of the world, and I would bear personal testimony to the remarkable influence of this rural Baptist chapel and its people. I was part of the Mainstream team that held regular meetings here in the early 1980s. I was privileged to host some consultations at Gorsley during my presidency of the Baptist Union in 1986-87. In recent days I have greatly enjoyed the stimulation of sharing in some of the Word and Spirit Leaders' conferences. This is truly a church with a gift for hospitality and a heart for people.

The genius of the Christian Church is in its durability, diversity and inclusiveness. The turbulent beginnings and the subsequent history of Gorsley Baptist church is an intriguing story. That a church came to birth in such unpromising soil as 'Heathens' Heath,' as it was deservedly nicknamed 200 years ago, is evidence of the love of God and the life changing nature of pragmatic Christianity. It is also a tribute to the perseverance of a group of mission minded Christians in a sparsely populated region.

I have known Pat and Beryl Goodland as family friends for forty years and they have been an inspirational encouragement to me in my ministry. During the 20 years that Pat was at the suburban Stanmore Baptist church he was a constant source of ideas and imagination for a younger generation of ministers. No one was more surprised than Pat when he received God's calling to move to rural Herefordshire.

The gifts of the Goodland family provided a crucial departure moment for the ministry of Gorsley Baptist church and this family in partnership with the church, laid some strong foundations for a significant period of spiritual growth and development.

This story of church growth and development bucking the national trend, especially in the last quarter of the twentieth century, is appealing. The mobilisation of the church in evangelism, and the practical tasks of involvement in imaginative rebuilding and extension programmes, will give encouragement to those who wrestle with needful change at the beginning of the third millennium.

Many churches have an open door ministry to their community. The unique factor at Gorsley is that they minister to a wider community through such projects as the Haven family centre, the Wye Valley Christian Festival and the ever-popular leaders' days. Under John Lewis's leadership the story of Gorsley continues.

This is an everyday story of ordinary Christians setting aside their gifts and talents for God's service. May the telling of their story be the means of inspiring others to attempt great things for God.

David Coffey
General Secretary of the Baptist Union of Great Britain
Moderator elect of the Free Churches

ACKNOWLEDGEMENTS

I would like to acknowledge the many friends who have helped and encouraged me to write this slender volume.

To the minister and deacons of the church, for ready access to the church records, together with members and friends who have allowed me to interview them, and to some who have permitted me to tell part of their story.

To the Rev David Coffey, general secretary of the Baptist Union of Great Britain, a colleague and friend for many years, for his very gracious Foreword.

To Peggy Lucas (nee Cox) for the generous loan of the personal memoirs of her brother David.

To those who have delved into their archives and produced photographs and drawings that capture the imagination and illuminate the text, Eric Beard, Gordon Bright, Mike Cole, Reg and Beryl Cox, Sam Eedle, Evangeline Goulding, May James, Betty Jones, Philip Price, Mike Tookey and Beryl Goodland.

To my hospitable friend Andy Meek, for providing facilities when my computer decided it could no longer cope with this manuscript.

To my candid and reassuring friend Lilian James, for reading and commenting so helpfully on the early drafts of this story.

To my encouraging friend John Fitzroy, for his literary skills and journalistic expertise so generously shared throughout the project.

To my talented artist friend Jim Shakespeare, for his landscape painting for the cover.

To my wife Beryl, my friend for over fifty years, who has encouraged, read and re-read each revision methodically and offered fair and constructive comment.

To these, I offer my warmest thanks and appreciation.

I also offer my thanks and sincere apologies to those who have shared their own memories and pictures, which have not been included. Inevitably, the abundance of material far exceeds the space available.

Patrick Goodland. Gorsley 2002

1

CHANGING SCENES

A warm summer evening in the middle of nowhere.

This is Gorsley, a quiet, picturesque village on the Herefordshire-Gloucestershire border, deep in the heart of rural England. The bees are buzzing, merrily collecting their life-giving nectar from the abundance of fragrant flowers. Dappled apples hang from laden, stooping branches. The sunlight dances down the hillsides, painting meadow flowers with vivid colours. The sheep idly graze and occasionally bleat plaintively.

Yet as the birds swoop and flit from hedgerows and well-dressed trees, there is a movement of a far different kind in the narrow, twisting lanes. On this lovely August Bank Holiday Sunday evening, cars creep bumper to bumper towards the Baptist chapel. Adjacent orchards and meadows are already covered with line after line of cars. Yellow-jacketed stewards continue to pack them into every available space.

It is the fourth day of the Wye Valley Christian Festival. So far, 4,000 people from all points of the compass have been attracted to Gorsley. They have come from cities and towns, villages and hamlets. The prolific flower arrangements in the chapel are magnificent. The floral artistry and Biblical promises they reflect whisper messages of encouragement, hope and inspiration. Amid the cascading colours that flood the church, many visitors have been enriched in spirit and emotionally refreshed. *Activate*, a vibrant programme of events for young people, has run alongside an action-packed *TraX* timetable for children. Twenty-five global missionary agencies have displayed graphic insights into their work among the disadvantaged people of the world. Morning

Bible expositions and evening music concerts have all been part of the fare on offer.

The country market produce stall has done a roaring trade. A thousand pounds of fresh runner beans, 400 pounds of apples, over 400 pot plants and sprays of cut-flowers, as well as 750 jars of honey, home-made marmalade, chutneys and jam have been sold. Countless meals, ploughman's lunches, tempting puddings, non-weight watcher's sweets and afternoon cream teas have been served in the restaurant and cafeteria. An abundance of books, greetings cards and crafts have tempted many customers. Several villagers have generously opened their gardens for viewing. Many garrulous gardening tips and ideas have been exchanged.

Tonight, the festival is continuing with its popular Songs of Praise. A giant marquee spreads like a massive mushroom covering the capacious chapel car park. Queues of people stretch out from the 'big-top' entrance to the surrounding narrow lanes. It takes 45 minutes to pack everyone into the arena. The sides of the tent have been removed to accommodate the overflow. Amid the music and singing there is a definite air of expectancy. One of America's best-known Christians is the principal speaker tonight.

As the sun sinks in the west, into the spotlight steps smiling former White House aide, Dr Tony Campolo. Here is the man who confronted ex-President Clinton about his involvement with Monica Lewinsky. This intelligent, hard-hitting university professor and Baptist preacher not only counselled the President, but regularly advised him on a range of social issues, including the serious problems affecting America's inner cities.

This is Gorsley August 2001.

The middle of nowhere feels more like the centre of the Christian universe on this idyllic evening.

But it wasn't always like this.

Two hundred years ago it was known as 'Heathens' Heath!'

2

FLOWERS AND THORNS

The county of Herefordshire was and still is to some extent a border county. Historically, the Brecon Beacons and the Black Mountains standing solid to the west, with the Malvern Hills to the east gazing down protectively on the hillside town of Ledbury, made travel beyond this county difficult. Gorsley rests comfortably in its own sleepy hollow. To the stranger or unfamiliar delivery driver, it is a maze of intersecting lanes, paths and tracks through woodland orchards and meadowland. From Linton Ridge you can observe the contrasting beauty of the village with its multi-coloured fields, its many narrow lanes twisting and turning, rising and falling. The scenery is constantly enchanting and changing. The hedgerows are seasonally speckled with wild roses white and pink, wild parsley, bindweed, strawberries, blackberries and moon daisies.

Gorsley, teetering on the edge of Herefordshire and Gloucestershire, is a place of natural beauty. Its name originates from the gorse bush, which used to be prolific in this area. William Cowper (1731-1800) in his poem *The Task* could have been speaking of our village when he wrote,

> *The common, over grown with fern, and rough*
> *With prickly gorse, that, shapeless and deformed*
> *And dang'rous to the touch, has yet bloom,*
> *And decks itself with ornaments of gold,*
> *Yields no unpleasing ramble.*

The red soil is famed for its fertility. Flowers and fruit were profitable crops until the middle of the 20th century. Increasing imports, labour costs and cheap airfreight gradually caused the demise of this local industry. In the spring, the damp meadows and open woodlands are carpeted with snowdrops, wild daffodils and bluebells. The stone walls and hedges frame these golden floral displays. The English bard William Shakespeare in *The Winter's Tale* expressively describes the scene: '*Daffodils that come before the swallow dares, and take the winds of March with beauty.*' In the early months of the year, the clear-voiced thrush and blackbird fill the air with their joyful singing. The warbling and flitting of the wren from branch to branch on the skeleton trees is distinctive. Later, the trees are decked in their blossomed spring clothes, competing with the resurrection new life of hedgerows, running thorny brambles and bursting colourful bushes. The recurring seasons of the year all bear God's signature. The changing pageantry of nature's scenery is the visible garment of our creator. '*Earth's crammed with heaven, and every common bush afire with God.*' (Elizabeth Browning, 1806-1861, from *Aurora Leigh*).

There is little obvious form to our village. It is definitely accessible and has overlapping and inter-penetrating communities. It lacks a cohesive centre, having neither a village green nor a main street. Houses are clustered in small groupings or isolated on the undulating hills. It does boast a Post Office and shop, The Roadmaker pub, an Anglican church, Gorsley Goffs primary school and the Baptist chapel.

Glancing eastward, the large Gorsley stone chapel stands prominently in a central position to the homes of its residents. This is the meeting place of Christians known as Baptists, though today when thankfully denominational allegiance is less important, the congregation is eclectic. To understand why such a large chapel was erected, it is important to mention where the label Baptist, for a cluster of Christians, has its roots.

Early pages of the New Testament speak of John the Baptist baptising by full immersion as a sign of repentance, spiritual cleansing and commitment to God. As the Christian movement spread, believers' baptism was one of the recognised ordinances of the church. In the course of time, variations occurred in the mode of baptism. It is not possible to date these variations and changes with exactitude. Some have tried to claim an 'unbroken baptismal succession,' similar to the claim by other Christians in regard to 'apostolic succession.' Both are unproven and most unlikely on practical as well as historical grounds.

During the 16th century Renaissance and Reformation, many Christians sought to free themselves from moribund and superstitious religion. The Bible became increasingly available in European languages. Groups of Christians sprang up in western, central and northern Europe, covenanting with God and each other by celebrating believers' baptism and the Lord's Supper. Religious persecution in England sent many like-minded believers scurrying to the Netherlands.

In 1611, a small group of British Christians headed by Thomas Helwys returned from Amsterdam to England. They formed the first independent Baptist/Congregational church in London. By the 1620s, the movement had spread. They separated themselves from the Church of England, with its episcopal structure, and practised the baptism of believers who had made a conscious choice to be disciples of Christ.

Baptist Christians were some of the first to demand freedom of conscience in the interpretation of the Bible and to obey the perceived teaching where it was in conflict with the state. Today, this is expressed in terms of separation of the church and state. Inwardly, Baptists believe that the authority of the church is the result of Christ's Holy Spirit dwelling in each believer. The church meeting is the structure ideally led by the Spirit of Christ, through prayer, Biblical principles and interactive fellowship.

The persecution of minorities and of non-conformists came to boiling point in England and Scotland during the reign of Charles 1 (1625-1649). He was beheaded in 1649 after a disastrous reign ending in civil war. Oliver Cromwell and the Commonwealth period (1649-1660) managed to bring some stability. This was an expansionist time for non-conformity. Charles 11 (1660-1685) was a frivolous and unprincipled man. With the Cavalier Parliament, he seemed to have a mania for persecuting religious minorities.

Parliament introduced four Acts, which have a direct bearing on our story. In 1661 the Corporation Act compelled all municipal office bearers to be members of the Church of England. The Act of Uniformity (1662) decreed that all ministers, clergymen and schoolmasters should declare their belief in everything contained in the Book of Common Prayer. This drove an estimated 2,000 Christian leaders out of the Church of England. The Conventicle Act (1664) and the Five Mile Act (1665) forbade the holding of religious meetings other than in churches and expelled non-conforming ministers from coming within five miles of a town. These four measures are popularly known as the Clarendon Code.

As a result of the Act of Uniformity, the rector of Weston-under-Penyard and Hope Mansell, John Skinner, walked out under protest. He went down the road and gathered together a group of like minded non-conformists. Sitting on barrels and probably drinking their local brew of cider, they planned their next move and formed themselves into the Ryeford Baptist church in 1662. We know that a Baptist chapel was built in that village well before 1700. Weston-under-Penyard is situated approximately six miles south of Gorsley and three miles from Ross-on-Wye.

It was from Ryeford that these zealous non-conformist ministers came to Gorsley, preaching the gospel of Jesus Christ. In the original church minute book, in splendid copperplate hand writing, we have John Hall's account of the beginnings of Gorsley Baptist church written on the 29th November 1831:

'The precise time when the gospel was first introduced into this neighbourhood is now uncertain. But it is well known that more than forty years ago, Mr James Williams, then pastor of the Baptist Church at Ryeford, visited Gorsley, and preached the gospel of the kingdom for several years with frequency and zeal, and individual instances of success. Mr Williams left Ryeford in the year 1801 and was succeeded by Mr Micah Thomas, now of Abergavenny, who also preached frequently at Gorsley, during the four years he continued as pastor of

Ryeford. He was succeeded at Ryeford in the year 1809 by the present pastor, Mr William Williams, who continued these labours of love at Gorsley, endeavouring to pass the light of spiritual instruction into the minds of the thoughtless and ignorant, and instrumentally to turn them from darkness to light and from the power of Satan unto God. He continued to preach at Gorsley without money and without price from 1809 till 1819.

By the labours of these successive pastors of Ryeford a good congregation was gathered, several persons were converted to God, through his blessing on their efforts, baptized, and received into the church at Ryeford; many of whom are fallen asleep in Christ, and those that remain, still members of Ryeford, are by reason of age and infirmity, expecting soon to depart hence and be no more seen.

The worship at Gorsley was conducted first, at a house called the Stillworks; but the congregation increasing this was found too small; and a large Room was procured at a house called Blindman's Gate, for which the church at Ryeford, though poor themselves, paid a rent of thirty shillings annually, and where their present pastor continued to preach till the year 1819. Oftimes in the summer when this large room would not contain the people attending, Mr Williams preached under a tree in the garden. But about this time the church at Ryeford apprehended they should be under the necessity of withdrawing their Pastor from Gorsley, to preach startedly at Ross, in connection with Ryeford; yet anxious that Gorsley should not be abandoned, they agreed to solicit the Trustees of the late Mr Goff of London, Messrs, Boyce, West and Sockett, to take to Gorsley as one of their stations, for preaching the gospel and keeping a Free School.

The Trustees agreed to do so, on condition of the church at Ryeford, paying two years Rent of a House at Gorsley for this purpose. This arrangement being made they sent a Preacher to commence his labours in March 1819; and at the expiration of two years, their present place of worship was erected (the older section of Gorsley Goffs school) *some persons were baptised and a church was formed.*

This first pastor of Gorsley however, soon showed himself to be an awfully immoral character and his name shall not be even mentioned in this history. He was dismissed and succeeded in June 1823, by Mr John Jones of Monmouth. Under his ministry several people were baptised, and added into the church. But at length an unpleasant altercation took place between him and some of the members, and much confusion ensued, which we deem much better to suppress than permanently to record. He left in March 1830, and was succeeded by the present pastor, Mr John Hall, 23, in January 1831. Mr Hall being made useful, several persons were baptised, and these, with some old members to the number of twenty, were reorganised, and formed into a new church, on the 7th of September 1831. The congregation now increased, and manifesting much attachment to their minister, Mr Hall was ordained to the Pastoral Office, on the 29th of November 1831.'

The Edward Goff Charity has played a significant part in the development of the spiritual and educational progress of the village. Edward Goff was born in 1738 in a thatched cottage just south of the country village of Huntington on the north-western borders of Herefordshire. A man of rural simplicity and with little formal education, he followed his father into farm labouring. He developed a strong constitution, a reflective mind and a personal, practical Christian faith. At the age of 25, he walked the 150 miles to London and found employment as a coal heaver on the banks of the river Thames. Growing industrialisation created an expanding demand for coal and made it a profitable boom industry.

Goff, frugal and shunning luxury, eventually became a prosperous and respected merchant in his own right. In London, he mastered the art of reading and taught himself to write. When 73 years of age, it gave him great pleasure to teach a young friend to read. He was most liberal in support of many charitable institutions and gave generously to the poor. He supported numerous Christian ministers of various denominations, whom he counted among his friends. He died in 1813, leaving the residue of his estate to trustees, with clear directions that it should be applied to promote, or to establish, schools in Herefordshire or neighbouring counties, for the education of poor children. Not only was education for poor and neglected children provided at Goff schools, but for many years, the trustees, in accordance with Edward Goff's ideals, connected their schools to the preaching of the Christian gospel. Under the usual arrangements made by the

Gorsley Goffs school, the original chapel.

charity, it was customary for the schoolmaster to also be the village pastor.

The trustees of the Goff Charity built the first chapel and school building in Gorsley in 1821. It is still an integral part of the Gorsley Goffs primary school complex.

The girls of Gorsley Goffs school 1905. Headmaster Mr J. C. Shambrook.

3

THE UNFOLDING SPRING

Pastor John Hall's influence in Gorsley is legendary. Born in Minsterley, Shropshire, on 29th November 1805, he belonged to the 'poor but honest' commoners. His elementary education was in rudimentary dame schools, which was as much as his parents could afford. Possessed of good natural abilities, he was of cheerful temperament with an active and retentive mind. He had a thirst for knowledge and an unquenchable craving for learning. He was converted to the gospel of the Lord Jesus Christ in a local Methodist meeting, through the convincing preaching of a young woman. John Hall's honesty and integrity were sustained by his devotion to a study of the Bible. These qualities, coupled with

Rev John Hall (1831-1881).

formidable willpower and a strong voice, made him a good choice for the social roughness of the times. Epictetus says: '*He is a wise man who does not grieve for things which he has not, but rejoices for those which he has.*' By this reckoning, John Hall was a wise man for he majored on his strengths. His gifts for public ministry were recognised and confirmed by his fellow Christians and he became a regular on the preachers' plan.

On 27th June 1827, John Hall married Sarah Heakin and settled in her home village of Pontesbury. The arrival of their child in June 1828 was not only a cause for great joy but it became a catalytic experience for John. Should they have their child baptised as an infant? His prayerful study of the scriptures demonstrated to his satisfaction that Christian baptism was a rite of passage to be offered only to those who had intelligently responded to faith in Christ. His conclusion involved him in a double decision. His infant should not be sprinkled and he himself should be baptised by immersion. He joined six other people who became the founding members of the Pontesbury Baptist church. It was not in his nature to dispute or dogmatise with people of differing views, but he consistently proclaimed Baptist principles of churchmanship for the remainder of his life.

His preaching and warm pastoral gifts were also recognised when the Goff Trust invited him to minister in a full-time capacity in a small cause at Cherbury. His aptitude for study and learning added to his knowledge. The Rev John Richards, who observed him in his early days, wrote to a friend: *Being young, strong and willing to work, he had a full share of preaching appointments, which he conscientiously supplied, regardless of distance or weather.* The Goff Trust in January 1831 sent John Hall to Gorsley. Subsequent events were to prove that their prayerful direction was very profitable for the kingdom of God in this vicinity.

Likeable and kindly enough in their fashion, Gorsley folk, in common with most villagers, had likes and dislikes. In the 19th century, the area was not nicknamed the 'republic of the lawless' without reason. Gorsley common, or 'Heathens' Heath' as it was sometimes called, was a veritable maze of footpaths and cart tracks, anticipating our now tangled network of narrow roads. A tough pioneering spirit was essential to endure in the harsh conditions that prevailed. Undoubtedly there were petty squabbles, family feuds, brawling, drunkenness and considerable sexual promiscuity.

John Shambrook, headteacher of Gorsley Goffs school (1876-1919) and a deacon of the Baptist church, commented in 1886 that at the beginning of the 19th century, '*Gorsley was ecclesiastically a sort of "no man's land." The inhabitants were generally without knowledge, without church, chapel, school, or any refining influences whatever. Their sabbaths were spent in cock-fighting, football, an old fashioned game called wickets, and in drunkenness and fighting. An old resident informs me that a Sunday rarely passed without five or six free fights occurring...horse stealing, sheep and pig stealing, and other offences of a like nature were of frequent occurrence, and during the first ten years of Mr Hall's residence in the place, from six to ten persons were annually transported from the locality.*' By the time John Hall settled in the village in 1831, many of the squatters and settlers would have established themselves, having paid small sums to buy out the manorial claims, converting their leaseholds to freeholds. Their houses were rough basic structures consisting of a stone or brick chimney stack, and a wooden frame wall filled with wattle work and then daubed with clay, mud or plaster. Young people applying for work, however, would still give any address other than Gorsley to their prospective employers, for the village was a synonym for unreliability.

Amid the murky social conditions, the poverty and the measured depravity, there were people of principle, honesty and truth, among them a growing number of Gorsley non-conformist Christians. They found encouragement as the youthful energetic John Hall and his wife settled into their ministry. The faithful had prayed for a leader who would unite them and they were not disappointed. The minister's first sermon set up a signpost as to the direction he was going to pursue in his new task. His text in a modern version reads: '*This is how God showed his love among us: He sent his only begotten Son into the world that we might live through him.*' 1.John.4:9. Gradually the message of God's love and his purposes of spiritual renewal for the individual and for the community began to penetrate the minds and hearts of the people. The church began to grow numerically. Mr Shambrook, a friend of the minister, reports in his *Life of John Hall* that, '*by the end of the first full year, the number of members had risen to thirty-eight and the church had become the centre of an active influence for good to the surrounding district.*'

Admittance to the membership of the church was on profession of faith in the Lord Jesus Christ as personal Saviour and Lord. Each candidate was interviewed. If evidence corroborated their profession of faith, then they were baptised by immersion and received into membership. In earlier years, this sacrament took place in a pond at the Stillworks. Within months of John Hall commencing his ministry, the church meeting decided '*that there be a Baptistry made in the Chapel.*' The necessary excavations took place and the task was completed on 14th January 1832. They wasted no time in putting their new acquisition to use. The next day the excited, faithful members witnessed the baptism of seven people. There must have been a cheerful water-carrying party, processing up the lanes with buckets of water filling the new pool. I wonder whose well was used? Gorsley Goffs is probably the only school in England where archaeologists in years to come will discover the remains of a Christian baptistry.

Later, the water carriers decided that there was a more expeditious way to fill the receptacle. Resolution 4 in the original church minute book records: '*Resolved that a well be sunk opposite the back door of the chapel, which was accordingly done October 1832 and a pump set therein the following spring.*'

In these formative years, John Hall surrounded himself with committed men who shared his enthusiasm and concerns. They were not men of great formal education, nor men of leisure, but men of the soil who toiled with their hands. Educated in God's school, they applied God-given wisdom to their everyday experiences. They obviously were not always in tune with the pastor's struggles, but their motives were always pure and they were open to persuasion.

John Baldwin, a skilled woodworker, was a man of original thought, sterling principles and a loving disposition. He died in 1866 after 50 years of consistent living and great activity in the cause of Christ. A trustee of the Goff Trust, Mr Jonas Stone, was present once when he preached. He remarked: '*John Baldwin's sermon was as clear as rock water and would have shamed half of London's doctors.*'

James Hartley was an excellent Sunday school worker and for many years a deacon and treasurer of the church. An entry in the church minute book records: *'He was the father of this cause, his life was circumspect and his end was happy.'* He died 28th December 1839.

The most educated and intelligent associate of John Hall was George Aubrey, an agricultural machinist, inventor and shopkeeper. He was the pastor's confidant. He served as a Sunday school teacher, deacon, local preacher and treasurer. He was a generous man who on a Saturday evening would look over his coins to find the brightest and the best to place in the offering plate. His motto was, *'Only the best is good enough for God.'* He bore his final protracted illness with great courage and died 8th February 1882 in his 70th year.

Growing congregations of fallible human beings inevitably have potential problems. The infant Gorsley Baptist church had its casualties. During that period, society was often unmerciful in its application of the law and harsh sentences were handed-out for what in today's world would be considered minor offences. This spirit was sometimes reflected in the church. Its discipline was strict and unyielding. Exclusion for a period from the Lord's Table was not uncommon. Compromise was considered to be weakness, but disappointment, sorrow and love for those who failed to live-up to their profession are expressed frequently in the original church minute book. These random entries reveal that a stern discipline was imposed (the initials bear no clue as to the person's identity).

1836 March 20, GH excluded. For being pregnant by her husband before their marriage. This female we thought one of the most pious in the church.

1836 November 2, EF excluded. For a case of illegitimacy. Such was this girl's hitherto amiable conduct, that this circumstance afflicts and overwhelms us all.

1845 June 18, CD excluded for ill usage of his wife, and other acts of immorality.

1853 March 9, PP excluded for criminal intercourse with another man, she was detected by her husband; and on his evidence expelled. Her general behaviour to her husband is bad.

1858 March 31, AB excluded for improper familiarity with a single female woman and refusing to appear and answer to the charge. This man has been nothing but a nominal Christian.

1872 Oct 2, WW excluded for neglect of the means of grace. This woman has a fine tongue but is full of deceit.

These early non-conformist Christians set themselves high standards and faithfully sought to reach them by prayer, regular reading of the scriptures and self-denial. They walked miles to share fellowship and attend services. They gave out of their poverty to support the work of God in Gorsley, counting it a great day when they resolved *'to allow our pastor the sum of five pounds a year.'* This would be in addition to his salary of £50 per year from the Goff Charity for his leadership in the school.

The minister's involvement was expansive. He was the village schoolmaster as well as the pastor. He visited the sick and cared for the dying. He preached passionately and set himself high standards in his preparation. Often, he would be called upon to write last wills and testaments, not only for his own flock, but also for others of different persuasions. He was a trusted man. His physical strength led him sometimes to be impulsive. Remonstrating with a man who was habitually drinking too much, the offender turned on him in an offensive manner: *'Don't ya know I'm in tha 'abit of kickin people who do poke their nose into my business.'* *'Oh you are, are you!'* said John Hall, *'then kick me.'* He turned his back towards the aggressor to help the operation. It was probably the minister's renowned strength and courage that tamed the boasting assailant.

Numerous stories have been handed-down of the influence of this worthy pedagogue-cum-minister, John Hall. Some doubtless are barnacled with embellishments over the years. One anecdote, which has substance, tells of a visiting assize court judge in Gloucester expressing surprise and satisfaction at the absence at his court of any major crime from Heathens' Heath. This was attributed to the influence of the minister's preaching and caring presence. There was a spiritual discipline in learning and loving, to which every member had to be committed. An entry in the minute book of the 18th November 1841 gives clear instruction: *'Every member of this church shall meet in classes in the different districts in which they reside for their spiritual improvement and to promote brotherly love.'* So the contemporary emphasis on house groups is no new phenomenon!

In a desire to foster adult education, the church established a circulating library in 1836. The minute book records: *'in aid of which we are much indebted to the kindness and liberality of the Baptist friends at Ross.'* This cause was further advanced by: *'Resolution 10. At a teachers meeting held on January 1.1837 resolved that a penny a week subscription in aid of the library be entered into for one year.'* A penny was no mean sum in those years and is an indication of their eagerness for knowledge. A Bible society was also instituted to supply Bibles and hymn books at a cheaper rate through co-operative purchase. These people were generous and thrifty!

The Christian gospel is unequivocally committed to social involvement. Many years before the welfare state, John Hall led the church to form a friendly society, or benefit union, to care for the sick and to support the unemployed. The society became so popular that men from surrounding villages sought membership. Within a few years, over 300 people were on the members' list. The village pastor was the centre and soul of the society, which at one time accumulated several hundred pounds. That was a considerable sum in those financially hard times. They practised welfare support with commendable accountability. John Hall proclaimed Jesus as the redeeming Saviour of mankind, but he also saw clearly that Jesus gave himself in selfless service to others, taking a variety of forms according to people's needs.

The general lines upon which the church was to develop had been laid down and its organisation had taken shape before it moved to its new home. The increasing congregation had outgrown the original

The chapel about 1900.

chapel. They had moved to a room capable of accommodating 100 people at Blindman's Gate in May 1837. It had been fitted-up by Mr Joseph Keyes over his blacksmith's shop.

1851 was the year of the Great Exhibition. In London, the Crystal Palace had been built, treasures from around the world had been assembled and thousands of people poured into the capital to celebrate the achievements of Queen Victoria's British Empire and its industrial skills. In Gorsley, the Society of Protestant Dissenters called the Particular or Calvinistic Baptists meeting at Blindman's Gate, were beavering away clearing top soil, sinking a well, collecting lime, nails and money and excavating stone for a new chapel. In 1837, Gorsley Baptists purchased land on which the present chapel stands today. Its

The interior of the chapel in the 1950s. Note the oil lamp holders.

purpose at that time, however, was to create a burial ground. Neighbouring Anglican clergy refused to bury non-conforming Christians and their unbaptised infants. Prior to this purchase, the Baptists were forced to carry their dead six miles for burial at Ryeford. In buying God's acre, the church solved the burial problem and also secured enough ground for their mid-century new chapel. Commendable foresight is shown by '*Minute 12. On the 25 March 1837. Mr John Hall purchased a parcel of land near two roads adjoining William Hammond's premises as a Burial ground for the church to the amount of £20 which was paid for by public subscription, and now vested in trust for the use of the church.*'

The church members, many of whom were poor, gave sacrificially of their time, labour and money. Others contributed timber or stone, while still others provided horses and carts for transport. Mr Russell Pontifex laid the foundation stone on 7th May 1851. The completed

Part of the congregation in the late 1880s.

chapel was opened on 11th May 1852 when three services were held and three ministers preached. What powers of concentration, listening and endurance our forebears possessed! The total cost was £672.18.9d. By 1856, the whole debt was paid. The pastor wrote in the church minute book: '*O give thanks unto the Lord, for he is very good to us.*'

For the next 30 years, the Rev John Hall led the church, filling the chapel which had been built to accommodate 400 people. As early as 1859 it had been found necessary to erect at the west end a balcony capable of seating an additional 106 worshippers. The contract document measures eight inches by four inches and is the epitome of simplicity. It reads: '*Linton Augst 6. 1860. I hereby agree to erect a Gallery in the Gorsley Chapel according to the drawings & specification using the best materials of their respective kinds for the sum of £72.0.0. the whole to be completed within 2 Months from this date. Signed Ths Davis.*' This was a time of expansion. In 1857, there were 45 baptisms and in 1863 another 48 baptisms were recorded. 1856 and 1860 saw new developments as, with missionary zeal, chapels were built in Kempley and Crow Hill. Some years later, preaching stations were erected at Four Oaks (1887) and Kilcot (1934).

This enlarged responsibility seriously taxed the pastor's strength. He relinquished his responsibilities at the day school in 1864 and focused his energies on the church. In 1871 he suffered a stroke which deprived him of his speech for a while and forced him to rest. Later, heart trouble made it impossible for him to continue his conscientious, pastoral visitation of his people and in 1881 he tendered his resignation. In his letter, he wrote: '*My earnest counsel to you is that you keep yourselves together, fill up your places in the House of God and live in peace and love with one another, and especially give yourselves to prayer.*' He died in 1885. His successor, the Rev Edward Ashton (1881-1899) recorded in the church minute book: '*He was the father of all…his long pastorate and highly successful work won for him the esteem and affection of thousands.*'

Rev Edward Ashton (1881-1899).

Over 500 people attended John Hall's funeral. The Rev E. Edwards, who for many years had been associated with the beloved pastor as a fellow trustee of the Goff Trust, delivered an eloquent address. Included in his remarks he said: '*As a man, John Hall was a fine type of the straightforward, honest, outspoken Englishman. Politically he was a Liberal. Theologically and ecclesiastically he was a Protestant, a non-conformist and a Baptist; and able at any time to give a reason for his beliefs, while at the same time extending charity to those who differed from him. As a Christian minister he maintained a consistent character,*

One of the oldest pictures of the chapel taken from the rear of the premises.
Note the stables on the right and the mounting steps between the stables
and the rear hall.

*and that no easy task, for more than 50 years in the same place. He was
sympathetic and affectionate amongst his people and ever ready and able to give
them counsel in their business, domestic, physical, as well as mental and spiritual
difficulties'.*

4

PATTERNS AND BRIGHT COLOURS

The membership of the church continued to grow. A new magazine entitled *Our Own Illustrated Monthly* was launched in 1893. In that year also, a new manse for the minister and his family was acquired. There were property sharks back in those days and the vendor proved to be of that turn of mind. His forged deeds in respect of Ashcroft, Manse Lane, went undetected until 1895. When the rightful owners filed their claim and investigations were made, it was discovered that purchasers of other properties had also been misled. The legitimate owner, on hearing that the church had been defrauded, generously withdrew an action in Chancery and settled the matter for £100. This was a relief to the church, the sum being about half the original purchase price. This episode was a severe blow after so much money had already been raised for the manse. It was softened by generous gifts from sympathetic friends, including the widow of the renowned preacher Charles Haddon Spurgeon.

By the end of the century, Gorsley had been somewhat morally reformed. The chapel was acknowledged as a centre of village social life for many. Chapel members and folk with no religious persuasion mingled together, generally in harmony. But change was afoot. The new century brought new discoveries, new ideas, bicycles, motor cars, buses and trains that were destined to break down the isolation of country life. The movement of progress and change began almost imperceptibly, but throughout the 20th century accelerated at an ever-increasing rate, bringing in its wake new challenges to the church. The Rev Henry Cross (1899-1909) brought sensitive order and organisation to the fellowship. Mr George Forty was appointed as the first church secretary to keep minutes of all church and deacons' meetings, a task which Mr Hall had performed. Official notepaper and communion cards were introduced. In 1906, it was *'decided to order one dozen bottles of unfermented wine for communion and to keep the remnant of the other kind for cases of sickness or necessity.'* What was this 'other kind' of life-enhancing elixir which had previously been used for communion? It sounds like an

Rev Henry Cross (1899-1909).

exhilarating drink, but the church minutes are silent about the recipe of this alchemical preparation. In the same year, a coach house was built at the manse for the minister's horse drawn vehicle. For this building, the deacons authorised an expenditure of £4! For the well ordering of the large congregation, the first seat steward and sidesmen were appointed.

At the beginning of the new century, the deacons unanimously agreed *'that a musical instrument be suggested to the church as needful for sustaining our public worship.'* The introduction of new music and instruments will always produce animated discussion. We can be sure that the chapel congregation would have 'chewed the cud' on this suggestion. This was a gravely and emotionally charged issue. Until then, praises had been led by Mr Francis Adams, as precentor, equipped with his tuning fork, with the assistance of Mr John Roberts and Mr Charles Marshall, with their flutes. A large and enthusiastic choir occupied the gallery, ensuring harmonious singing of hymns and anthems. The organ was installed in 1900, but on the first day it was used, Mr Adams sadly died. Two years later, after more passionate

Rev Henry Cross and the deacons. (1905?).

discussion, the organ was dispatched to the gallery, presumably to be in greater harmony with the choir.

After a decade of consistent ministry, the Rev H.R.Cross left for pastures new. A tribute to his popularity is recorded in a local newspaper account of his colourful send-off. *'After a series of interesting farewell services, the Rev H.R.Cross, of Gorsley Baptist Chapel, finally left the neighbourhood on Thursday morning last. His departure was the occasion of a very novel and interesting scene. The young men belonging to the chapel secured a low carriage, which was gaily decorated with flowers, and took it to the manse gates, and when the Reverend gentleman and his wife had taken their seats, a snapshot was taken. About twenty young men then took hold of the ropes attached, and drew the carriage to Newent station, a distance of four miles. The journey was made merrily by the singing of 'For he's a jolly good fellow,' &c., and by the hearty cheers of the children of the Gorsley church school and the Newent schools as the procession passed along. A great number of lady members of the church and congregation also escorted their pastor and his wife to the station. On reaching Newent, Mr Cross addressed a few words to his old friends, and thanked them for the grand send-off they had accorded him. They then boarded the train for Ledbury, and amid cheers the train steamed out of the station.'*

Mr Cross's successor, the Rev Stanley Cox, began preaching as a boy in Wales. After training at Wycliffe College, Oxford, and a pastorate at Kings Stanley, he was called to Gorsley in 1909. In the contagious spirit of patriotism of 1914, the Rev Stanley Cox joined the Royal Army Medical Corps. His Christian caring principles found full expression on the bloody battlefields of France. As hurricanes of shells came crashing-down on the infantry in the muddy, slimy trenches, he ministered to the wounded and dying. He returned to Gorsley in 1919, a man broken in health from illness contracted in the trenches. With ailing strength and amid much suffering, he drove himself on in his compassionate ministry, making a

Rev Stanley Cox (1909-1926).

deep and lasting impression in our village. A man of evangelical zeal, he endeared himself to the congregation. He combined thoughtful preaching with strong pastoral gifts. To many, he was a beloved and devoted pastor. An extract from the 1925 annual pastor's letter and balance sheet is typical of his concern and love for the people. *'I feel very thankful in that I have been able to come into touch with you in your homes during the year. This service has been a privilege…do let us all expect great things from God, and prayerfully labour for them to be realised.'*

Characteristically, Mr Cox introduced a series of meetings for the deepening of spiritual life. He moved the poorly attended midweek harvest service to a much more attractive annual Sunday celebration. The Monday harvest auction was a jolly and boisterous event which the late David Cox, the pastor's younger son, graphically describes in his memoirs. '*The final rounding off of the bountiful year took place in the chapel vestry on the evening following the Harvest Thanksgiving Sunday. A coal fire burnt fiercely red in the iron grate, two large hanging oil lamps shed light and added extra warmth to the crowded room. The heat brought out more of the pervading odours of the fruit, flowers and vegetables arranged behind the stalwart bearded figure of old Fred Chapman. He in the 1920s was the officiating functionary at the Dutch auction of the produce. A prayer would be said and the assembled company would give vent to their feelings with a vigorous rendering of "Bringing in the sheaves". The room seemed overcrowded with atmosphere and people, but no one minded, least of all old Fred, as he warmed to the task and mopped his face with a red spotted handkerchief. Bidding was brisk and generous and the first fruits were normally disposed of at a price acceptable to the proud donor. The depleting display grew smaller and smaller until at last only the centre piece remained. This symbolic wheat sheaf of bread had been made by one of our two local bakers.* (Clem Aubrey, whose wife was also the village postmistress, and Ernie Fishpool, who lived with his sister Alice.) *No one would dare to speculate which one. By tradition this last item was 'put up again' by the successful bidders until at last the bidding would be closed, the sheaf cut up and shared among the multitude. Proceeds from the sale would be shared among the needy in the village.*'

History was again made when the church commissioned its first overseas missionary. Miss Dora Cracknell served in China with the China Inland Mission, now renamed the Overseas Missionary Fellowship. In 1911, Mr Cox, in a desire for greater accountability, introduced an annual balance sheet and pastor's letter.

Anniversary celebrations were highlights in the routine of chapel life. They were occasions when new hats would appear, often decorated and occasionally given to fruitful or floral extravagance. They were

Mrs Stanley Cox and the ladies' committee. (1916?)
Back L to R. Mrs Bert Chapman, Mrs Harriet Jones, Mrs Reg Jones,
Mrs Roberts, (unknown)
Seated: Mrs Jones (Kempley), Mrs Geo Goulding, Mrs Stanley Cox,
Mrs G. Forty, Mrs Sam Goulding.

kept in place with vicious-looking hat pins. Many of the men wore floral button holes regularly on Sundays. The in-season flower was kept fresh by a subtle water container which clipped onto the lapel. Anniversary days would have seen an array of special floral decorations, brightening the otherwise dark suiting of the male members of the congregation.

Sunday school treats, often known as the 'May-tea' even when celebrated in early June, were appreciated in days when most rural entertainment was of the homespun variety. After home-made ice-cream and brightly-coloured pop had been dispensed from Aubrey's wagonette, there were races for modest prizes, rounders, musical arms and other games. At the end of this junketing, children scrambled for sweets liberally scattered all over the farmer's borrowed field, regardless of hygiene. These simple pleasures closed with the singing of the

Floral hats were in vogue in the 1890s congregation.

doxology, '*Praise God from whom all blessings flow, praise him all creatures here below.*' David Cox recalls in his memoirs when the Sunday School outings became more expansive. ' *"The treat" took the form of an outing to May hill by horse-drawn wagonette, an excursion which I remember with keen delight, the rather bumpy journey through winding, leafy lanes jogging slowly along between the hedgerows without a care in the world, our eventual arrival, climbing out of the wagonette in our eagerness to clamber up the hill, the magnificent panoramic view when we reached the wooden crest through bracken as tall as I was, the shells we found telling of another incomprehensibly distant age. We were in Gloucestershire now and could clearly see the city and the winding Severn; beyond lay the Cotswolds and Cleeve Hill, to the north the Malverns reached into Worcestershire and further still was the high country of Monmouthshire and glimpses of the beacons of Brecon. The home fare provided for our refreshment tasted good in the open air and we played our games with added zest. The wind soughed gently in Queen Victoria's Jubilee pines and once*

The choir master Bert Chapman and his worthy steed. (1914?)

more that afternoon I experienced a sense of having captured a memory that nothing could take away.'

Some years later, to the expressed delight of the fellowship, Stanley Cox's eldest son, the Rev Reg Cox, entered the ministry. He served conspicuously in Warley, Birmingham, and later held a responsible post in education. During Stanley Cox's ministry the names of Mr A. E. Chapman and Mr and Mrs Arthur Clifford surface in the records. The former was the accomplished choirmaster, while Mr Clifford was the chapel organist and celebrated gravedigger. Mrs Clifford gracefully prepared the communion table for 40 years! They were authentic Gorsley characters and undertook many practical roles in the fellowship, being admired and deeply appreciated.

Les Aubrey, whose grandfather George Aubrey was the close confidant of John Hall, recalls that when he was a boy Mr Cox would visit the Post Office home owned by his parents. The pastor would sit on the dining room table and invariably reach for the bottle of smelling salts which stood on the dresser. This seemed to ease his gassed weakened lungs. Despite his physical weakness, he and Mrs Cox would entertain groups of children at the manse at Christmas. Sadly Mr Cox died in 1926 at the age of forty-one and was mourned by many.

The abbreviated ministry of the Rev L. G. Schofield (1927-1930) is notable for its outstanding preaching and for the manner of its demise. Eloquent in the pulpit, he was perhaps a little unwise in his subject matter. He took frequent opportunities to scold the village for its partiality to liquor of the intoxicating variety. In those days, cider was brewed on many a smallholding. It appears that this contentious divine banged his drum to one tune too many. His opinions did not fit in harmoniously with his flock or the wider community, so the old village custom of 'tanging' was evoked. Organised by one or two of the more forceful leaders of village opinion, the campaign

Rev L G Schofield (1927-1930).

was carried out by a number of men assembling outside the offender's residence in the late evening, with an assortment of pots and pans. They then began to bang away heartily on their improvised drums for an hour or so, before dispersing, only to reassemble at the same venue night after night, hoping for the speedy departure of the unwanted one. This barbarous treatment was perhaps a hangover from the days of 'Heathens' Heath.' I can vouch for its authenticity, having had conversations some years ago with a friend who personally witnessed this cruel expulsion. I sincerely trust that no member of the chapel was involved in this intimidating and repulsive practice.

In a Baptist church, the minister is financially supported and released to do his work by the congregation. The choice of a new pastor is outwardly a democratic affair decided by the church meeting. Ideally, the community of believers gathers together to interpret and administer the business of God and to determine the will of the Lord for the congregation. The choice of the next minister rested on the splendidly named Havelock Roderick, a Welshman with twinkling Celtic eyes and a good preaching voice. He came in 1931

Rev Havelock Roderick (1931-1953).

The Rev Havelock Roderick and the deacons in the chapel centenary year 1952.
Standing L to R: Percy James, R H Goulding, Ken Goulding, Arthur Jones, Harold Goulding, A. Forty, Arthur Clifford.
Seated: Mrs F. M. Cox, R. C. Goulding, Sam Goulding, Pastor H. Roderick, Bert Chapman, R. E. Jones, Miss B. Keyse.

and served the church and community, together with the Herefordshire and Gloucestershire Association of Baptist Churches, until 1953. The new minister started a men's meeting, originally to bridge the gap between Sunday school and the church. Also in this period, a women's meeting was commenced. Its president was Mrs George Goulding.

The church celebrated its anniversary in 1932 with special services. The minute book records: '*An immense tent was erected in the chapel grounds which consisted of a framework of wood, covered with a dozen rickcloths. In it, upwards of three hundred people sat down to tea.*'

It was during the 1920s and 30s that noticeable changes occurred in transportation to the chapel. Mr Brookes replaced his horse and trap with an early Morris Cowley. His daughter, Mrs May Goulding (nee Brookes) of Holders Farm, has the distinction of being the first person to drive a motorised vehicle onto the chapel turf. Reg Jones, from Waterdines, Oxenhall, who drove his wife Madge to church in

May Goulding (nee Brookes) on the left,
with the first car to be driven on to the chapel turf.

Reg Jones and his sporty three wheeler Morgan runabout.

a sporty three-wheeler Morgan runabout, soon followed her. As the stables and mounting block fell into disuse, a parking ground became essential. The carrier's cart gave way to Bayliss' bus service which in turn was swallowed-up by the Red and White bus service, running from Monmouth to Gloucester, via Ross, Gorsley and Newent. The village blacksmith was trying to adapt to being a motor mechanic. Some of the brighter sparks among the young men were striving to fathom the miraculous workings of the petrol driven electric dynamo, which could provide domestic lighting.

Les Aubrey humorously recalls that at a time when very few cars came through Gorsley, the only two people who owned them were Colonel Kirk, of Linton Hall, and the esteemed Dr Johnson, of Newent. The colonel's wife was taken ill so he sent someone, presumably on horseback, to call the family doctor. Some time passed. The impatient military man thought the doctor was being rather dilatory. He set off in his vehicle down his tree-lined drive at some speed, but just as he was approaching the iron gates Dr Johnson swung into the drive and great was the resulting crash. The red-faced colonel and the winsome

The chapel choir outing to Cheddar 1925.

doctor were unscathed. I am led to believe that their friendship remained unsplintered.

The Second World War (1939-1945) saw an influx of evacuees from cities into the tranquil countryside. The ferocity of the Nazis Luftwaffe's bombing of cities like London, Birmingham and Liverpool was such that Britain could not risk losing more of its children. Packed into third class railway carriages and pulled by hissing steam locomotives, the children were bundled off to safe pastures. It is difficult to imagine the reaction of little children, being uprooted from their homes and terraced houses and arriving in the wide-open spaces of Gorsley. They came with large manilla labels tied around their necks, often with only their personal evacuation registration numbers stamped on them, their few clothes tied in a parcel, and their gas masks.

They had been used to the constant noise and bustle of city life, increased by the commotion of war-wailing sirens, anti-aircraft guns and exploding bombs. They came into a world of relative quietness and of unimagined experiences. Cows providing milk, bleating sheep and skipping lambs, the hoot of night owls and the chattering of roosters and hens. Billeted in cottages and farms, they attended Gorsley Goffs school. It was all disturbing, exhilarating and sometimes emotionally upsetting both for the evacuees and the hosts.

The chapel played its part in welcoming these young strangers. The minister was involved in shepherding these additions into the community. A few older children adapted well to the new environment and never returned to their former homes. Once the aerial bombardment began to ease, a steady stream of children returned home to their more familiar urban surroundings.

Another of Mr Roderick's notable achievements was the introduction of an annual singing festival held in Hereford each Good Friday. Choirs from around the county's churches filled the galleries of Commercial Road Baptist church, while the congregation packed the main body of the building. A great feast of choral music was enjoyed as rich Welsh minor tunes mingled with more traditional and well-loved familiar hymns.

5

STRENGTH FOR TODAY AND BRIGHT HOPE FOR TOMORROW

The centenary of the chapel building was celebrated in May 1952. A week of meetings attracted large congregations to hear a variety of speakers. Among them were the Rev Reg Cox, son of a former pastor, the Rev Frank England, for many years a missionary with the China Inland Mission, and the Rev Theo Bamber, pastor of one of the largest London Baptist churches and a well-known speaker at the Keswick and other Christian conventions. The ministry was rich in spiritual challenge and anticipation of the work which lay ahead for the church in the future. Mr M. E. J. Hobbs, a teacher at Newent secondary school and a member of the church, wrote a short history of the chapel. He surveyed the influence of the chapel in the village over the years. He also drew attention to the changing culture when, in the closing paragraph, he said: '*Once the chapel was overcrowded, but now there are empty seats, for many people in Gorsley, as in England, have left the faith of their fathers.*'

Both Mr and Mrs Hobbs gave unstinting service to the children of the community. They left the district in 1952 to take a new educational challenge in East Africa. Pastor Roderick retired in 1953. To him had fallen the duty of leading the church through the years of blackout, rationing and sorrow during World War 11. He had faithfully served the church, community and the Herefordshire and Gloucester Association of Baptist Churches for 22 years.

Britain was still recovering from war wounds and shortages when the new pastor, the Rev L. G. Stapleton, and his family, arrived from Birmingham. The year, 1954, saw the lifting of war restrictions, which ended meat rationing. It was also notable for a major post-war Christian evangelistic campaign led by a comparatively unknown American evangelist, Billy Graham. Thirteen thousand people packed a sports arena each evening in Harringay, North London. A full coach party went up from Gorsley. The 13-week campaign reached a fitting climax with a capacity congregation filling Wembley football stadium. Such was the interest and publicity that 'religion' became a nation wide talking point. Gorsley was not untouched. Numerous members and friends

Rev L G Stapleton (1954-1960).

attended the crusade and were spiritually renewed with all that they heard and experienced.

Mr Stapleton introduced family services, using his considerable artistic talents to illustrate the stories of the Bible. These were years when the Sunday school movement was very active in Great Britain. Five chapel Sunday schools in Gorsley, Kilcot, Four Oaks, Crowhill and Kempley attracted over 200 children to their classes each Sunday. Mr Stapleton introduced a corporate annual celebration, when all five schools united for a festival. Lilian James, who participated as a child, recalls: *'This was a fantastic time of encouragement and fun, tea parties and games at Gorsley School followed by a 'crocodile' marching in step in twos up to the chapel singing, "We're marching to Zion." Then followed wonderful singing, the children having been trained by Mr Stapleton on a rota basis in their various Sunday Schools for the previous months. Those of us who were part of this, both teachers and children, talk of it still.'* An appreciable number of baptisms and additions to church membership were recorded in the late 1950s.

For years the church had been talking of the possibility of a new hall, toilets and kitchen. Social functions had often necessitated the cartage of chairs, crockery, cutlery and kettles from the chapel to Gorsley Goffs school. It was with a sense of delight and relief that the younger members of the congregation saw their minister backing the cause for more modern facilities. On the site of the old stables and trap shed, where, as late as 1950, horses chewed over hay while their owners worshipped in the chapel, a new church hall, together with toilets and kitchen, were erected. The drains for the new accommodation were dug laboriously by members, and the indefatigable Arthur Clifford battled through tons of Gorsley stone to form the septic tank. The oldest member, Mrs George Goulding, and a young Sunday school scholar, Stephen Timbrell, officially opened the hall in November 1959. Years later, Stephen became a leader and deacon of the church.

As an added bonus, mains water had arrived recently in the village. Previously, three hours of hand pumping had been necessary to fill the baptistry from the outside well. The water was conveyed into the building via a system of wooden viaducts, through specially tunnelled apertures in the wide walls of the chapel.

On 3rd October 1959, a valedictory service was held for Miss Pearl Griffiths, daughter of the Sunday school superintendent of Crowhill. She was the second lady missionary in the history of the chapel to serve overseas. Her place of appointment was Raxaul on the borders of Nepal and India, where she worked as a pharmacist with the Regions Beyond Missionary Union. Mr and Mrs Stapleton with their family, having received a call to a church in Albany, Western Australia, emigrated in 1960.

The Christian church in Great Britain was losing members in the uncertain 1960s. The advent of mass television communication and the 'never had it so good' philosophy of the politicians led the nation into a materialism unmatched in the country's history. The then church secretary, Mr. R.C Goulding, in one of his annual reports, spoke of the *'plodding years.'* His analysis was a result of devoted service and experience. He diligently served the church, first as treasurer and then as secretary, for 47 years unbroken service. His foresight in securing the playing field and adjoining land next to the chapel is a constant reminder of his vision. Could he have anticipated the day when the field would be literally packed with the parked cars of those attending special events in the chapel? Thankfully, he lived long enough to see it. His contribution to the West Midlands Baptist Association was considerable, while his knowledge of churches and people was encyclopaedic.

The chapel has had the privilege of many long-serving officers. For the first 50 years, the pastor undertook all the correspondence. Mr George Forty then became secretary for 30 years, followed by Mr R. E. Jones (Betty Jones' father) who was in office more than 30 years. Mr R. C. Goulding was next in line, to be followed by his nephew, Mr L. Keith Goulding, who served for 22 years until his retirement in the year 2000. He was succeeded by David John.

Five Gouldings honourably cared for the treasury of the church over a period of 90 years. They were, in order of appointment, Mr Daniel Goulding, Mr George Goulding, Mr R. C. Goulding, Mr Reg H. Goulding and Mr Ken Goulding. A break with the family tradition occurred when Mike Howley followed Ken Goulding as treasurer. This task was becoming more onerous as congregations and giving increased. After 10 years of dedicated commitment, Mike handed-over this office to Lewis Jones, a retired bank manager. He brought his single-minded skills to the task, with Graham John developing the chapel's computer system to its current high level of technological sophistication. When Lewis retired in 2001 and moved to South Wales, Steve Booth was appointed treasurer.

With several preaching chapels in its care, the church has been fortunate to have a number of lay preachers. Ken Goulding, a respected farmer, family man and a long-term deacon, was a gifted preacher for

Ken and May Goulding.

many years. His sermons reflected his careful reading, meditation and daily prayer. Each morning after milking his herd of cows, followed by breakfast, he would retire for an hour to study the Bible and his books. This discipline, together with his gracious personality, was the key to his thought-provoking ministry.

Unfortunately, his farm became a casualty in the 'foot and mouth' epidemic of 1967. The disease was discovered on a neighbour's farm. Ken had been advising the owner, Mrs Savage, since the tragic death of her husband four years previously. Ken's animals were not infected, but, because of his contact, the Ministry officials insisted on slaughtering his 500 animals. In a newspaper article, he said: '*As we walked down the straggled line of condemned cows contentedly munching their daily ration of sugar beet tops, there were times when I had to turn away from the valuers to hide my emotions.'* Expressing appreciation for the support of his friends and neighbours in this traumatic experience, he went on to say: *'I would like to add that my sincere desire and prayer is that you who are stock owners may be spared this unpleasant experience. If the loss of my animals helps to this end, I am quite happy to bear with any injustice you may think has been imposed upon us.'*

Ken Goulding's courteous demeanour in the face of this tragedy was an eloquent affirmation of his God-centred spiritual resources. He proved in adversity the truth of the words in one of his favourite hymns,

> *'When all around my soul gives way,*
> *God then is all my strength and stay.'*

Reflecting the social climate of former days, the leadership of the chapel was generally male-dominated until the 1980s. Many fine and outstanding Christian women, though not office bearers, have had a significant influence within the fellowship through the quality of their spiritual and practical lifestyle. It is invidious to select a name or two, but it is necessary to illustrate the major contribution women have made to the ongoing commitment of the chapel to believers and non-believers through the years.

The New Testament missionary pioneer, Paul, speaks of a colleague's mother as *'your mother and mine.'* Such a woman was Mrs George Goulding (1874-1963). She was affectionately known as the mother of the Gorsley chapel congregation for the first half of the 20th century. Her wisdom, generous listening skills and astute counsel, cemented

Mrs George Goulding.

Brenda Monkley with her mother Kathleen Holmes.

with loving grace, gave her unsought status with the congregation. Another deeply appreciated and caring lady was Mrs Harriet Jones, who delivered the monthly magazine faithfully for many years in the Four Oaks and later in the Upton Bishop areas until 1950.

Kathleen Holmes, the mother of Brenda Monkley (wife of the Rev Douglas Monkley) was brought up in Gorsley. In her teens she went into service in London and was given training as a cook in a wealthy home. She was encouraged to attend a Baptist church, which offered her a warm welcome and supportive fellowship. On returning to Gorsley after World War 1, she married and, with her husband, settled in Prospect Row. Kathleen was to live there contentedly for the rest of her life. Her husband had been gassed and made a prisoner-of-war, which caused him to suffer for the rest of his life. They enjoyed a devoted relationship. Generosity and genuineness were her character garments. An indefatigable worker among young people, she led the young men's Bible class and various other youth activities.

Every night before retiring to bed, she knelt in her small living room and prayed individually by name for each young person in her various classes. She kept open house and an open cake tin for *'our dear young people.'* A woman of limited means and formal education, her influence upon the former younger generation of Gorsley's indigenous children is abiding. As one local lady remarked, recalling how Mrs Holmes was her confidante in times of family trouble: *'You told her all your secrets and then she would throw the key away!'* I recall visiting a house in the village during my early days as minister. The woman declared rather abruptly *'We be church.'* I then dropped Mrs Holmes' name into the conversation. *'Ah,'* she said, *'She be ma best friend, even though she be chapel.'* Her winsome gift of friendship and understanding made Mrs Holmes a valued friend, a patient listener and a life enhancer.

'More things are wrought by prayer than this world dreams of. Therefore let thy voice rise like a fountain for me day and night.' (Tennyson). Women of prayer have contributed deeply to the wellbeing of the chapel family and its influence on society over the years. Mrs May James is one of God's treasured intercessors. It is not the rhetoric, the eloquence or the logic of prayer, but how fervent and believing our prayers are that matter. Prayer is the pulse of life, which leads us into gracious action. For May, this is translated into generous kindly deeds. For many years, her sensitive visitation programme, often bearing thoughtful gifts of flowers or fruit from her garden to a wide variety of people, has brought inspiration and encouragement at a time of need. If Christianity is more caught than taught, then May James is spiritually infectious.

'Should I go on? There isn't enough time for me to speak of…who through faith, fought and won. They did what was right and received what God had promised.' Hebrews 11; 32-33. We salute the memory of those who have served God faithfully and well and thank God for the inheritance they have passed on to succeeding generations.

In the 1960s, the popular press began to question the relevance of the church. The Bishop of Woolwich issued an episcopal paperback,

May James.

Honest to God, which attracted enormous publicity. It became a best seller when it was previewed in a Sunday newspaper with the headline, *Our image of God must go*. It sold a million copies in 14 languages. Bishop John Robinson and his fellow travellers were gifted people who were trying to bridge the gap between the church and the world. They certainly caused people to think. Their thesis seemed to suggest that God was intellectually superfluous, emotionally dispensable and morally intolerable. Journalese in style, the book appeared to be an attack on traditional values and a Biblical understanding of God as a supreme and existing eternal being.

These were difficult days nationally, and rural churches did not escape the tensions and the struggles. It was in these turbulent times that Pastor Mervyn Evans continued a faithful ministry of Biblical exposition for 13 years (1961-1974). He came as a bachelor and left having married the district nurse. Both were pastorally caring and concerned. In the autumnal days of November 1962 an evangelistic campaign under the banner *Come Back to God* was held. Led by the Rev Dennis Paterson and the Rev Bernard Dodd, the meetings were held in the Crowhill chapel and at Gorsley. In the 1960s, a new manse was built in the shadow of the chapel. Ashcroft, the former manse, was sold, new housing properties were being built, mains electricity had arrived and in 1960 the M50 motorway sliced its way through the northern boundary of the village.

Rev Mervyn Evans (1961–1974)

6

LOVE AND LABOUR

In 1800, four-fifths of England's population lived in villages. Today that is reversed with four-fifths of the population living in urban areas. The demographic change gradually affected Gorsley following the second World War. Until then, the majority of families were often large, hard working, relatively poor and static. In the 1980s, I corresponded with Charles Hartley, who had emigrated to New Zealand as a young man with two of his brothers. Jim, Alan and Charles became sheep farmers. Their other brother, Walter, remained in Gorsley and was a gracious pillar of the chapel congregation. Charles was always thankful that he had spent his early years in Gorsley and expressed his deep appreciation of the influence of the chapel on his life. Born in April 1892, he lived well into his nineties. He retained clear and vivid memories of younger days.

'I am now an old man,' he wrote, 'but I am so thankful for God's great goodness. I was brought up to work. I was one of eight children, four boys and four girls. We all had our jobs to do. I had to take the milk round Gorsley before I went to school. I had a big can I carried the milk in. I measured the milk out at the door as people wanted it in pint or half-pint measures, which I carried with the can. I used to go from Poplar farm up to Gorsley and a few houses around the school and Gorsley church. I don't remember being paid for the milk, I think they paid by the week or month. Then I walked to school, walked home for dinner and back to school for the afternoon.

My dear mother worked hard to clothe and feed us. There was no electricity in those days. We had to cut wood and dry the kindling wood in the oven to light the fire in the mornings to cook breakfast. Good old bacon cured by mother.

What a change from today. Mother cooked, washed and clothed us, never a spare moment what with making clothes, mending, churning the cream, making the butter and all the other jobs she did. Mother made our bread, enough for a week at a time, in an old fashioned oven which you heated-up by wood. You made the fire in the oven and then swept the ashes out and put the dough in while the oven was hot. She often made cake with the same dough.

There were horses of all sorts, great heavy drafts to small ponies. The ponies were used mostly to draw small gigs or traps or to ride on. Then the larger farm horses did the heavy work such as ploughing and cultivating and lots of other work which had to be done in the course of a year. There was no machinery like we have today. Men started work at six in the morning and came home at six in the evening. The ploughman on Mr Goulding's farm was paid 12 shillings a week. He had a wife and a large family to keep as well as rent. I have often wondered how they lived on so small a sum of money. Transport to the railway station was by horse and cart. The heavy draft horses carted loads to the station to be sent on the goods train.

There was such a lot done by manual labour in my younger days. Harvesting was done by hand, men cut the grass by scythe then the mowing machine came in. We used to build the hay into hay-stacks and thatch the ricks with wheat straw. Also the corn was cut by sickle and crook and tied by hand. Most people who had a bit of land grew a patch of wheat and harvested it into a stack and thatched it. When the threshing machine came round to the farms, they would get it tracted and the wheat was ground into flour. Most people had a couple of pigs. They would buy them at weaning time which was about seven to eight weeks old, mostly they would get the small ones because they would be cheaper. They usually did well and grew into good bacon pigs, which was a good help to a working man and his family. Butter was about a shilling a pound or under, eggs around a shilling a dozen dependent on the time of the year, bread was very cheap. I have had some ups and downs through my life, but I don't think I am any the worse for it, its taught me many things.'

Homes were often small and poor in the village in the early years of the 20th century. May James, born in 1913 the youngest of 10 children, recalls that they were poor but happy and enjoyed wonderful

Percy and May James's wedding on the 24th December 1933.

security in their parents' love. Typically, many men would have been classified as casual labourers. May remembers her father rising at five each morning to collect water for the family from the well some distance from their cottage. He was a man of many skills and sought work wherever it could be found. At various seasons he would find employment as a council roadworker, cracking stones for road making, helping on farms, fruit gathering, wood cutting and dynamiting local quarry stone which was used for house and wall building. Every evening he tended his large garden until nightfall, providing all-the-year-round vegetables and fruit for his family. The annual cured pig provided bacon, ham and fat. Mother baked bread and delicious lardy cake once a week in the capacious cottage wood oven. All clothes were hand washed, scrubbed and pressed by flat irons heated on top of the range fire.

Many families had a weekly bath night. The galvanised tub was brought in from the washhouse and placed strategically near the open fire. Mother and father would collect additional water and heat and fill the bath, and one by one the family would step in for their personal ablution. These were labour intensive days in the cottages of Gorsley.

The Post Office, as today, was a place for exchanging news and views. If only the walls could talk! Both Mr Warren, the head teacher, and Miss Sally Redfern, a schoolteacher, lodged there at various times with Clem Aubrey's family. Mr Warren was a disciplinarian. *'They did used to cane us on the hand if we misbehaved, but it did us no harm, probably some good,'* says Les Aubrey with a twinkle in his 90-year-old eyes.

The fruit and flower season was always a busy family time. Clem Aubrey would have his children up at 5am, picking cherries until school time. Among his numerous part-time jobs he was a fruit trader. During a reasonable season he would buy-in fruit from smallholdings and local gardens and transport the produce to Gloucester on his horse-drawn wagon. Such was the abundance that it was often necessary to make the journey three times a week.

As late as the 1970s, the clashing of steel and the popping of guns at the crack of dawn during the cherry season could be heard. Sheets of galvanised metal were hung from trees. By an ingenious network of strings pulled by Perce Johnson, of the Tump, the clashing, clattering steel proved an efficient bird scarer in Harold Wadley's orchard opposite the chapel. The rooks and blackbirds didn't like the cacophony and they shot off the branches as though propelled by rockets. It was primitive, intermediate technology, labour intensive but effective. It was a step back into more sublime times of village life.

It is easy to rhapsodise about earlier days in the countryside. The joys, imaginary or real, of the simple life, must be tempered with realism. Life was often more relaxed but there were also many hardships. A traditional village supportive spirit, however, was very evident in former years. Almost everyone in the village was related. Interest in the family, for whatever motive, was maintained. Today, a changing population, smaller families, dysfunctional families, business pressures and the insularity of modern life, all contribute to a lack of cohesion within community village life. The young, influenced by the contemporary, instant, 'me-culture,' are often isolated from their parents by thought forms and fashions. As the previous moral fabric of our country becomes unravelled, villages do not escape the consequences. One of the challenges facing the Christian church is to help build a caring and supportive community in the 21st century.

7

LORD OF THE CHANGING YEARS

The concluding 25 years of the 20th century saw immeasurable shifts in rural culture. Increased mechanisation in farming techniques meant that fewer people were employed on the land. 75% of farms in Great Britain were now worked by the family, often father and son. Unemployment and genuine poverty increased as many indigenous workers had problems in re-training. For centuries, villages were small communities where people knew each other and assisted each other as the season's work required. In the 1960s the motorway created ready access to our village and opened it up to commuters. This radically changed the demography. 'Incomers' now form the largest part of a village population. Many who work in cities or towns consider a car journey of an hour to the work place to be a fair price for the reward of living in a physical environment of peace and beauty. Retirement in the country can be for many couples an idyllic anticipation of glorious views, bubbling brooks and docile, furry animals. It can also become a nightmare of loneliness when a partner dies. In the National Census data of 1991, the population spread of Gorsley was found to be in the following categories.

Under 16s	83	(16.5%)
16-44s	186	(36.9%)
45-64s	154	(30.6%)
65s +	81	(16.0%)

66.7% were employers, managers and non-manual workers, of whom the majority travelled to work by car. There were about 185 households within a two-mile radius of the chapel. 25% of the working population in 1991 were still directly employed in farming, though this figure was declining. The last 20 years, while welcoming new 'incomers' into the community, has seen a marked decrease in the original indigenous rural population.

Agricultural man may still wear his cloth cap and get thoroughly bronzed or rain-soaked as he farms the land in all weathers, but his tractor now usually boasts an all-weather cabin and often a hi-fi radio which brings constant information and music as he ploughs the field. He is often well acquainted with world trends and is 'radio street wise.' To exist in the rural area, with severely depleted public services, he needs a decent car. His knowledge of, and dexterity with, complicated machinery and techniques make him a skilled craftsman.

In the midst of this maelstrom of increasing change, I was invited by the church in 1976 to become its next minister. In 1974 I had presented a paper to a national conference of church leaders on the subject of church growth and outreach to the community. During the robust questioning time which followed, a rural vicar thanked me for my contribution but said, '*The principles of caring, sharing and teaching the truths of the Bible, which you have found successful in the London suburbs, would not work in a rural situation.*' I thanked him for his contribution and had to acknowledge that I had no experience of ministry in a rural setting. That man became for me a

Rev Patrick J Goodland MBE
(1976–1994).

disturbing influence! The challenge stayed with me and when the Gorsley invitation arrived two years later, I knew I had to respond positively. Our suburban church had seen considerable numerical

Minister and deacons during the 150th church anniversary celebrations 1981.
Standing L to R: Peter James, Mike Howley, Keith Gooch, Ron Goulding,
Alf Beard, Alf Watkins, Derek Wadley, David John.
Seated: Wilf Goulding, Keith Goulding (secretary), Patrick Goodland (minister),
Ken Goulding (treasurer), Geoff Jones.

growth and consequent extensions to the premises. My leadership colleagues, mostly businessmen and dedicated to church growth, were genuinely concerned that I was going to bury myself in the country, effectively cutting myself off from a wider ministry and reducing my stipend appreciably.

Feeling the inward call of God, we accepted the invitation in the knowledge that Gorsley was in the midst of a population and social change. The church had assured us that they recognised the need to reach out to the community. So we left our warm-hearted north London suburban church with apprehension, but with assurance that God was leading us and took-up the challenge of a rural pastorate.

We knew the area reasonably well as we had enjoyed many happy family holidays, staying in our caravan at Holder's Farm in Oxenhall. Ken and May Goulding and family had become very good friends. I had also occasionally preached at the church. We had proved the Lord's faithfulness and provision in the city and now we were entering into another faith adventure in the countryside.

To wrestle in autobiography can be disconcerting. The twin dangers of exaggeration or lack of objectivity can befog the actual situation and the precise circumstances that prevailed at the time. But let me paint the canvas *'warts and all'* as I saw it during my 18 privileged years of working in rural ministry.

Inducted as pastor on a very hot day in July 1976, the airless chapel was packed with people. It was a rather lengthy service and I remember being somewhat apologetic to some of our male guests as they left the chapel, not for the duration of the service, but for the melted varnish from the gallery pews which was now imbedded on the backs of their shirts! The abundance of delicious food and home-made cakes provided for the scrumptious tea was a foretaste of many such feasts in the ensuing years. Our guests returned home well fortified.

Some 85 people or so made up the morning congregation the next day. This was a third of the size we had left in our suburban church. I recall this came as a challenge and an incentive. This chapel had known better days, when many more worshippers of our living and loving God occupied the pews. *'Lord do it again,'* I silently prayed. God's purposes are always in terms of personal spiritual progress and numerical church growth. I naively proposed that we should have a moratorium of two years before any major changes were made. In the event, this became impossible through pew pressure.

Thomas Hardy's delightful commentary on village life in the mid-19th century still had a vestige of contemporary insight in the 1970s in Gorsley. *'The chapel members be clever chaps enough in their way. They can lift up beautiful prayers out of their own heads, they can,'* said Monk Clark with corroborative feeling, *'but we Churchmen must have it all printed aforehand'…. 'Chapel folk be more hand in glove with them above than we,'* said Joseph thoughtfully. In early visitation, I found that the general consensus was that the chapel people were generally exclusive, reasonably good folk, but living in a rarefied atmosphere. The introduction of some community sports activities, involvement in community-caring programmes, the young teenagers' Inglewood club, pantomimes and a splendid arts and crafts weekend, played their part in dispelling some of the real or imagined aloofness of chapel folk. The criticisms were not groundless. There are gaps in communication and misunderstandings in most communities. The tensions of involvement and separation in a rural setting can be real and difficult to solve.

The healing of perceived or real divisions was greatly helped by the Rev Geoffrey Cox and his wife June. As the incumbent of Christchurch, the Anglican village church, he and I were able to show our unity of purpose and our oneness in the essential practice of the gospel in the community. We had known each other in our London ministries and shared in the Westminster Fellowship, which was chaired by the Rev Dr Martyn Lloyd-Jones. One expression of local unity was an annual united churches three-day Bible convention. Nationally-recognised Bible expositors unpacked Biblical themes which stimulated deeper discipleship and devotion.

Sunday schools at Gorsley and at the four village chapels were still reasonably well attended in the early 1970s. The declining national statistics, though, were beginning to be reflected in our rural situation.

Youth work has always featured prominently at the chapel. A flourishing Christian Endeavour group is mentioned in the church records of 1905. The Band of Hope, a national temperance movement, was introduced before 1914. From 1920 to 1930, children's meetings were held at the Four Oaks chapel, instigated by Miss Mabel Goulding. After her marriage, Mrs Reg Jones, of Waterdines, took over the work. For many years, following the second World War, Floss Goulding, assisted by Lilly Millard and Sylvia Goulding, were leaders of the

Junior Scripture Union.

In Gorsley, Kathleen Holmes and Ruth Cole headed-up Comradeship, a children's missionary activity. In the 1960s, a youthful Derek Wadley led a thriving Young People's Fellowship. Its primary activity was a devotional meeting each Monday evening. The group continues today on a smaller scale and with a more varied programme. It is led by Jeff Goulding, himself a product of the overall youth programme of the church.

During the 1970s and 80s, a male voice choir brought together a variety of local men. As a group they were affiliated to the National Male Voice Praise movement. They participated in national rallies in London and Bristol, but their principal ministry was to support local churches and evangelistic events.

An aerial photograph of picturesque Gorsley 'resting peacefully in its sleepy hollow.' The chapel is in the centre of the picture.

'In the spring, the open woodlands are carpeted with wild daffodils.'

The first Inglewood club camp party explored London in 1977.

The interior of the chapel following extensive renovations in 1981-1982.

'Hidden Treasure', the theme of the flower festival 1991.

Thousands of visitors attend
the annual flower festival.

Flower festival 2001.

Marion Shakespeare (L) welcoming a Chelsea Pensioner to a festival, with Beryl Goodland and Jim Shakespeare. Jim and Marion enhanced the floral displays with their talented artwork for a number of years.

The impressive Tallowood Baptist church (Houston, USA) sanctuary choir outside the Gorsley chapel.

Fellowship meals help to build friendships

John Townsend's humour causes laughter to ring down the aisles.

Janet Gooch teaches a Sunday school class in Kempley.

Some members of the Beehive over 60s club enjoying the garden at the Copper Beech cottage.

Festival choir, conducted by Celia John, in full voice in 1991.

A morning congregation praising God in song (2002).

Les Aubrey and Betty Jones
reminisce.

Dr Tony Campolo
speaking at Festival 2001

Gorsley chapel has always known how to lay on a good spread.

8

BREAKING NEW GROUND

The 1960s have been described as *the decade of disillusion* marked by increasing cynicism and despair. The collapse of censorship following the Lady Chatterley trial, the rise of flower power, feminism and the acceptance of new lifestyles including homosexuality and liberal abortion, changed the moral landscape of conservative British culture. The Christian church was being shaken, perhaps as never before in European history.

In the 1970s, the troubled world saw war and terrorism in Ireland, Vietnam, Uganda, South Africa, Cambodia, Lebanon and a number of other countries. World oil prices quadrupled and North Sea oil came on stream. Britain joined the European Common Market and introduced decimal currency. Following a winter of social and economic unrest, Britain elected Mrs Margaret Thatcher as its first woman Prime Minister. High unemployment contributed to an evident social and moral decline. Divorce statistics, drug and alcohol abuse and abortions increased dramatically. The Queen celebrated her Jubilee for which the chapel organised special celebrations, culminating in a huge bonfire and fireworks display on the chapel field. Jubilee New Testaments were presented to every child in the vicinity.

Britain was experiencing a time of spiritual and Christian ferment. One million copies of the New English Bible were sold in a month, but there were disturbing patterns emerging. While traditional church attendance was floundering, many new religious and neo-orthodox groups were flourishing. The charismatic movement was gathering momentum as a reaction to dead orthodoxy. For some, this represented a threat. Others felt the church should be more involved. As pastor, I continued to plead for mutual tolerance and respect. The revered 18th century Cambridge preacher, Charles Simeon, said: *'The truth lies neither in one extreme, nor in the opposite extreme, nor in a confused admixture of both extremes, but at both extremes, even if we cannot reconcile them.'* We sought to recognise all that was good in this new enthusiasm, while holding to the centrality of Christ and his explicit teaching as the bedrock for belief and practice. Some in the new movement appeared to devalue the authority of scripture and elevate personal experience as a source of authority. This acted as a caution to us. We were united in believing that the Holy Spirit through the Bible conveys the truth of God to the church.

History bears witness to the birth of numerous and significant new religious movements, often doing an exceptional work at a particular time. Most in the end, however, have suffered from institutionalisation. Put in another way, these groupings begin with men and process to movements, then to machinery and end up as monuments. Not everybody in the chapel congregation would have been fully aware of this fermenting situation, but it was having its impact nationally and locally.

The British churches were also in the midst of a 'hymn explosion.' This was part of a larger movement of change in the style of worship practice. Modernised prayer books, Bibles, new hymnals and contemporary songs were knocking on the door seeking acceptance. The charismatic movement was pressing for a fresh approach to worship and advocating a more informal style. With the prolific output of new songs, it was inevitable that some were unbelievably banal in language and music, while others were very acceptable. It was the simplicity of words, harnessed to singable tunes, which could be picked-up easily and were memorable, that had instant appeal to a growing number of the younger people. Hymns and songs are for most Christian people the way they absorb their faith and truth. This places a sobering responsibility on those who select songs for worship.

These were not comfortable times for ministers and musicians! In

Mr and Mrs Clifford... dedicated church workers.

Gorsley, Arthur Clifford had been playing the harmonium for well over 50 years and had only been absent on 12 Sundays. Is that not worthy of an entry in the *Guinness book of Records*? Now in his eighties, he was failing and found difficulty in walking the few hundred yards from his White House smallholding to the chapel. Having arrived, he often had to be helped on to the organ bench. His once twinkling eyes were becoming inflamed and bleary and his fading eyesight restricted his choice of tunes to those he knew by heart. He couldn't abide the *Baptist Hymn Book* published in 1962. '*I reckon the best place for it,*' he said, '*is at the bottom of the quarry.*' In 1977 the church purchased a new electronic organ, but our dear old friend felt it was out of his range, so he retired. It was sad, but inevitable. My wife Beryl became the temporary organist. Through force of circumstances she remained in her 'temporary' role for 17 years. We were very grateful that she used her musical skills during those transitional years. She gave a sensitive lead to a growing variety of music used in our services and events and also accompanied the festival choir. It is a pleasure to see Stephen Beard on the organ and Christopher John playing the piano today. Both were young boys when we came to Gorsley.

Mr Clifford was a genuine Gorsley character. To listen to his stories of bygone years was an entertaining revelation. He had never travelled far from Gorsley. When I told him a man had actually landed on the moon, he would not believe me. '*Tha'll never appen,*' he kept repeating assuredly, '*never, never.*' We remember him fondly for his many contributions to the community as gravedigger, cider-maker, fence-mender and village carrier with horse and cart. He was a man of genuine loyalty to the chapel.

In the period leading up to Christmas 1978, he was manifestly physically very ill. With stoic determination, he sat in his chair by the open fireside in his cottage home, having experienced three heart attacks in as many weeks. Family and friends assembled the day the ambulance arrived. The trolley was rolled in, the attendants went to lift him, but he barked, '*Get out, get out of my house.*' He had no intention of going to hospital. Consternation gripped the assembled company. Then his niece spotted me standing at the door. '*The pastor will deal with this,*' she said confidently. Very uncertainly I moved forward, asking the friends to leave me alone with this man whom I admired. Kneeling down by his chair and holding his arm, I explained that we needed to take him to hospital for his own good and to allow his precious 'sweetheart' Florrie some respite. She was laying exhausted on her bed. Resistance to the idea began to fade at the mention of her name and need. I assured him I would go with him into the unknown and, for him, totally foreign territory of a large city hospital. I promised I would not leave him in Hereford if he was afraid or unsettled.

Quietly, I beckoned the attendants. Together we manoeuvred him into the ambulance. I cradled this dear old man in my arms the 14 miles to the hospital, reassuring him throughout the journey. Some hours later, I left him sitting in bed in the ward bathed, shaved and sweetly fragrant. As I slowly made my thoughtful way down the stairway, I offered a prayer of thanksgiving for Arthur and Florence Clifford, the National Health Service and for the Christian idealism that had inspired its creation.

On my visits to the hospital during the next few days, he opened his heart, expressing, very simply, his sense of peace and thankfulness. Among other issues, he gave me details of where I should look in his home *'for them there papers, my will, you know what I mean.'* His great concern was for 'his sweetheart.' She was now living with us at the manse and would do so for three enchanting months. A sweet, saintly and sensible rural lady, she had never travelled further than Cheltenham during her 80-plus years of life. She was wonderfully content and fulfilled. A policeman met me at the door of the church the Sunday following Arthur Clifford's admittance to hospital. He had died that morning.

I recount this story in detail to highlight some of the challenges the chapel congregation had to face in the 1970s. If the church was going to grow, it was imperative to grapple with new sociological trends. In our territory, there were numerous folk who were 'indigenous,' by which I mean they had been born and bred in the villages. Generalisations are notoriously difficult, but, from observation, genuine locals tended to be of independent mind, with a strong sense of family, tradition and continuity. In this group anyone middle aged and upward found any kind of change, and particularly change in chapel affairs, threatening and difficult to handle. It was perplexing that some of our farmers, who had exchanged their horses for 30 hp tractors, found difficulty in exchanging uncomfortable, worm-eaten wooden pews for more comfortable upholstered chairs in chapel. Why was great Uncle Bentwood's little, broken-beyond-repair squeezebox harmonium, given 50 years ago and unused for years, untouchable?

I have a deep respect and admiration for people born and bred in rural areas. Many of our older friends went through the frugal times of economic depression in the 1920s and 30s. They are sometimes individualistic, with a tendency to stubbornness and suspicion and frequently content to live fairly introverted lives. These qualities, I believe, are in some measure the result of environment, isolation and hereditary elements. These are not necessarily negative traits, but they need to be balanced by an understanding that, as humans, we are to consider progress and social community. In many areas of life we are our brother's keeper and share in responsibility for God's world.

Change is a fact of life. It is necessary and deeply challenging. The good management of change is crucial, especially in any voluntary organisation or church congregation. Autocratic leadership, which drives through change with ruthless disregard for people's opinions and feelings, can be not only hurtful, but also destructive. There is need for care and diplomacy, but also for corporate wisdom to know the timing and pace of necessary change. I would want to be among the first to acknowledge that probably I did not always make the right judgement as pastor. Hindsight is a glorious privilege!

Creative participation is one of the strengths of free church congregational government. Corporate decision-making encourages commitment. Through the years, this has been amply illustrated. The congregation has enthusiastically, and with great physical commitment, tackled many of the rebuilding projects. The financial cost of building and renovation has been substantially reduced by the outstanding involvement of so many talented members and friends. Two spin-off effects of physically working together are an increase in appreciation of each other and deepening friendships.

At this time, alongside the indigenous villagers, there was the ever-increasing number of 'newcomers' often designated as 'commuters.' Usually they were over 35 years of age and had worked long enough to reach a suitable salary scale to afford a new house, a modernised old stone cottage or a transformed barn in the country. The exacting demands of business, the need for relaxation and rest when they arrive home and the attraction of nearby town amenities, tend to isolate them from village activities. This mix of population, with its stress on individualism and self-fulfilment, will always be thought provoking to Christian groupings in a village, who believe in social obligation and integration. Many local young people were forced by lack of work or affordable housing to migrate to the towns. The result of the formidable changes in population balance meant there were challenges of a scale never before encountered by village chapels. New people, new circumstances and a new culture had grown up around us.

In 1977, we sponsored a community project – an arts and crafts weekend. We were amazed to discover the wealth of talent and interest in the villages. I remember knocking on doors, inviting people to join in the venture. Reactions ranged from incredulity and suspicion to enthusiastic support. In Kempley, I called on Allan Barlow, a farm employee and cowman. His children were members of our Sunday school in the village. I asked him if he had any hobbies or enjoyed crafts. He half jeered at me, '*You wouldn't have in the chapel what I make.*' '*Well, tell me about your hobby,*' I said. '*No, you can't be interested in what I do and if you dared put it on your display you'd get the sack.*' '*You let me worry about that,*' I retorted. '*Do you mean that?*' said Allan. Affirming that I really meant what I was saying, he took out several bottles of his finest country wines and we had a tasting session.

Samples of his hobby were displayed in the chapel, but, more importantly, he and his wife Chrissy came to the weekend celebrations.

Allan Barlow and his arts and crafts exhibits.

In his own words he says: *'When I went to the chapel I found so much warmth and friendliness. I had never known anything like it before and it made me think. I just felt I wanted to be part of it. I started attending the Sunday services and it was there that I heard the Christian gospel for the first time. I heard how Jesus had come so that we might share in God's abundant life. I heard how he could satisfy our innermost being, how he could make a real difference in my own life. I decided to commit my life to Him and become a Christian. The change in my life was pretty immediate. There was a peace and joy. I became more patient. I wasn't so self-centred and my tongue, which had been loose and vile, became controlled.'* Allan continues to be an active and dedicated member of the church.

Central to all the activities of the chapel fellowship was the well-attended midweek meeting. The evening commenced with praise and thanksgiving, moved to serious Bible exposition and discussion and was followed by a session of intercessory prayer for the community, the world and the church. This strengthened the fellowship by encouraging mutuality and accountability. It also formed the backbone of the church's life and mission.

As a church, we continued to review our situation. People's perception of Christianity, we discovered, was that it was irrelevant, dull and joyless, with a tendency to smug contentedness. Such comments were initially discouraging, but in a strange way they were also enlightening and stimulating. Some of us were obviously not projecting the right image! Was not Jesus physically strong, active in community, fond of food and parties, company and laughter? Didn't Jesus tell an occasional humorous story? Did his audience not smile at his innuendos? Using pictures, paradox, everyday objects, exaggeration and comparison as effective aids, he convinced people of the truth of God's love for them and for the world.

The car mobility of our rural population brought some painful challenges concerning our small chapels built in yesteryears, Kempley (1856) Crowhill (1860) Four Oaks (originally 1887) and Kilcot (1934). All were within a three-mile radius of our large centre in Gorsley. By long and historic tradition, the whole church family came together for a central Sunday morning service at Gorsley. In the evening, the congregation divided into five segments. Ideally, one would support the nearest preaching station to one's home in the evenings. The preachers' plan scheduled the pastor at each centre in turn. Numerous lay preachers spoke on other Sundays. This pattern had not changed since the Victorian era. This had been very appropriate when the general means of transport for the majority was one's own legs, or by horse and trap. Total attendance at all the five evening services in the mid-seventies rarely exceeded 60 people, often fewer. Clearly we were in a failing 'maintenance mode' and not in 'mission mode.'

Permission for the pastor to break with the Victorian tradition and to conduct evening services regularly at Gorsley was painfully extracted. One appreciated the emotional involvement of several of the longstanding members with their own small building. Some had been involved physically with the erection of 'their' building. The statistical truth was that very few people living around the chapels had come though the doors for many years, apart from Sunday school anniversaries and special occasions. Within a year of the change, the Gorsley evening service attendance trebled. New converts relished the variety of music and the opportunity for consecutive exposition of the word of God. This was, I believe, a most significant decision, a quantum

Then the guitars arrived! Tim Inchley (centre) leads a day seminar.

leap of faith, emotionally charged but essential for the progress of the kingdom of God. Biblical principles and patient pastoral work, together with fervent prayer and lengthy discussions, brought us through a straightened period of necessary change.

It was in the late 1970s, with more young people attending our services, that we reconsidered some of our patterns of worship. We noted that Biblical worship was often colourful and enthusiastic. Psalm 150 suggested that every known means of making music was used for the accompaniment of singing. The new wave of making music in our schools began to be reflected in our monthly family services. This proved to be the launching pad for greater variety and participation in our worship. Time spent carefully selecting new songs proved a sound investment. Sue Plowman, one of our young musicians, faithfully rehearsed our small, youthful orchestra. Songs and hymns from *Youth Praise* and *Psalm Praise* and a growing number of other books, became a part of our expanding repertoire. Then, the music group was born with guitars and drums. Their songs brought their own distinctive contribution to the monthly youth Sunday services and on special occasions. With deference to some older members of the congregation, the drums were muted!

The advent of the overhead projector ensured greater flexibility in the choice of material. A short period of singing before the evening service became an opportunity to introduce new and updated hymns and songs to the congregation. In the informality of this practice time, we were also able to encourage people to move forward and occupy the front seats of the chapel.

Hymnody is an essential part of congregational worship. The modernisation of language in worship, together with the increasing number of excellent hymns being written in the 1960s and 70s, prompted the church to introduce a new hymnal. Inevitably, this meant changes in language. Most of the older hymns use the 'thou' rather than the 'you' form of speech and many of them are dominated by masculine concepts. For these and other reasons we invested in *Hymns for Today's Church* which contained a balance of traditional and contemporary compositions. This became our basic book in 1982. For some, this was quite a radical change, but gradually the book gained acceptance by the majority of members.

Any attempt to examine the nature and shape of a local church in the light of New Testament teaching is to court unease. We are never invited to find an undisturbed security in an institution or in past achievement. The image of the church in the scriptures is often in terms of a dynamic body, a caring family, an excited bride or a conquering army. After much prayer for guidance and discussion in the fellowship of the church meeting, an overwhelming majority of members voted to launch an outreach and rebuilding programme entitled *Building for the Family*. We wanted to expand the ministry of the fellowship. From the outset, quality, consistency and continuity in ministry were our goals. Through consecutive Biblical teaching and prayer, we sought to have a deepening relationship with God. In every aspect of personal, community and church life, we desired that we

Bill and Joan Openshaw.

might become more Christlike in our lifestyle. We were gradually recognising that the mind, as well as the emotions, must be fully engaged in the mission to which God had called us in an increasingly secular world. Evangelism and social action were important subjects on our agenda.

We saw some significant conversions and additions to the chapel family. Bill and Joan Openshaw commenced their married life in northern England. They were enjoying a happy and contented marriage and had three lovely children. Bill had a secure and well-paid job, which enabled them to live in an attractive house. Life was pleasant, they had no great anxieties and they felt secure. All this was turned upside down when their youngest son, Timothy, developed inoperable cancer of the liver. Through the use of drugs and other therapies, his life was extended for a further two years. To the great sorrow of the family, Timothy died just after his fourth birthday.

The years that followed were difficult. Unresolved grief and perplexity undoubtedly were disturbing influences. They battled on as a family and seemed to be coping. Gradually, however, Bill became progressively depressed and withdrawn to such an extent that tensions began to affect their marriage, which eventually seemed doomed to irretrievable break-up.

It was at this critical time that Bill was offered a new job within the company in Gloucester. They seized this opportunity of a new start in a new location. It was as though they had been offered a providential lifeline to sort-out their problems. Initially, they moved into a property in Huntley, Gloucestershire. While it was a pleasant locality and they had good neighbours, neither of them could settle. They decided to look for another property. After a prolonged search, to the point where they were almost ready to give-up, they found a bungalow in Gorsley. When they walked into Pendle, they immediately felt this was the place for which they had been searching. In their own words, '*we had found our home.*'

A few weeks after moving into the village, gracious Kathleen Holmes knocked on their door offering them a copy of the chapel's monthly newsletter. She also gave Joan an invitation to a ladies' meeting at a neighbour's home. Wanting to meet some of the villagers, Joan accepted the invitation. Within weeks, the ladies had asked Joan to join them for a Sunday service at the chapel. She came and began to attend intermittently. Eventually, she felt able to encourage Bill to join her. But he was reluctant. For a number of years following Timothy's death, both of them had attended a church in Sunderland, near where they lived. Bill found the experience less than helpful and decided that when they moved he would have no more to do with the church.

Being a caring husband and wanting to rebuild their marriage and togetherness, Bill accompanied Joan to a morning service. In Bill's words, '*we both sensed something different about this church and so continued to attend fairly regularly.*' One Sunday, I was preaching from the gospel of Matthew chapter 7 and verse 7. I quoted the words of Jesus: '*Ask and it will be given you; seek and you will find; knock and it shall be opened to you. For everyone who asks, receives; he who seeks, finds; and to him who knocks, the door will be opened.*' When they returned home they discussed the sermon at length. Was this the key to understanding what life was about? Knowing God as creator and Jesus as Saviour? Was this the answer to their search for fuller life and a deepening human relationship with each other?

They decided that Sunday afternoon that they would take Jesus at his word. Kneeling together in their lounge, they prayed to God: '*Lord, we don't know what this is going to mean, but we know we want you in our lives. We want to be better people. Jesus come now into our lives.*' And as both of them say, '*He did.*' Through the discipleship talks, they learned more of Christ's way. Through the teaching ministry, they grew in Christian maturity and, through the Christian family, they experienced a strong relational fellowship with like-minded people.

Bill and Joan were baptised on profession of their faith on the 27 January 1980 and became devoted members of the chapel family. Both were active in the youth programmes for a number of years. Bill became a much-appreciated deacon and trusted leader. Joan had a fragrant ministry for 18 years, which included co-leadership of the Beehive club for senior citizens. They were dedicated house group leaders and both served on the pastoral/caring team, ministering to people both in the church, in Gloucester prison and in the wider world.

They retired in 1999 to Alnwick, Northumberland, to be near their sons and families. They are deeply committed to a ministry in the local prison, H.M.Acklington, sharing the transforming love and grace of the Lord Jesus with inmates.

Their story and similar testimonies demonstrate how God uses circumstances and ordinary people in his service. They also encouraged the fellowship to press-on in the task of making the gospel of Christ relevant and visible in a secularised world. Such transformed lives are part of the answer to those who are not convinced by words, but by the reality of genuine experience.

Commitment to anything long term is increasingly suspect in our mobile society. People are wary of getting caught up in activities which demand a change of lifestyle. We have sometimes been guilty of giving the impression to seekers that to become a Christian we are to cut off from former friends, healthy pursuits and relaxing hobbies and interests. That is a misconception. Our mission task is to believe in, and speak of, a living Saviour who transforms relationships and stimulates life in all its fullness. Long-term church members sometimes want to attach a whole package of cultural conditions onto new believers, which are inappropriate.

Gordon and Sylvia Bright owned and ran the village store, Post Office and garage in Kempley. Reading through our church newsletter, which was faithfully delivered to their home each month, Sylvia noticed that a group of men were erecting a hall and were in urgent need of a particular tool. When Gordon came in from the garage, Sylvia said, *'Gordon you've got one of these tools which the minister wants to borrow, can't you lend it to him?'* *'No,'* said Gordon, *'you know what churches are like, I wouldn't get it back.'* Sylvia was not defeated. She raised the issue again until Gordon picked up the phone and offered the tool. They were surprised when I said I would collect it in the next half-hour. They were even more impressed when a few days later I returned the implement cleaned and polished! This led to an invitation to the arts and crafts exhibition. I later learned that they closed the shop early that weekend in order to attend chapel.

This couple were among the early converts during our ministry in Gorsley. They were outsiders who became insiders. Their early steps into faith and joining the membership of the chapel highlighted the difficulty of transition. The problem was that representatives of the leadership wanted new believers to take on board a whole new sub-culture as a condition of membership. These included social attitudes,

Gordon Bright and his racing dogs.

a list of 'do's and don'ts' and behavioural patterns thought respectable for evangelical Christians. Rules and disciplines there must be, but a new convert should be accepted on profession of his or her faith in Jesus as Saviour and Lord. All change in lifestyle flows from the teaching of the word of God and the work of the Holy Spirit, recreating in the individual the image of Christ. An essential part of the church's ministry is teaching and nurturing people to spiritual maturity.

The problem about Gordon and Sylvia was that they kept and enjoyed dogs – racing whippets. Furthermore, these canine creatures usually performed well on Friday evenings at the Gloucester races. Wasn't gambling involved?

'*Pastor you must tackle this issue before you baptise them.*' I gently argued the case with some of the elders that their faith and conversion was the basis for baptism and not the issue of the dogs. '*Let's entrust any problems about ownership and dog racing involving gambling to the sovereign Lord who is well able to deal with this dilemma,*' I suggested.

Gordon and Sylvia were baptised and joined the fellowship. They became enthusiastic and generous members. Ah yes, the dog problem! We had recently commenced a Friday evening youth group and were desperately in need of help with the 40 or so lively teenagers who had joined the Inglewood club. They became members of the leadership team, which included Jackie Cole and Ron and Ann Goulding, and became committed partners and dedicated workers. The dogs were sold as the energetic young people's group took priority. Those were formative and growing years for us all.

Retired in Derbyshire, Gordon and Sylvia are still active in their village chapel and in community projects.

9

INCREASING LIFE AND GROWTH

Jesus, in his teaching, drew attention to common birds zooming in the sky and flowers snuggling in the grasses of the field. The deduction he made as he gazed at their delicate structure and exquisite beauty was profoundly comforting. *'Look at the birds of the air; they do not sow or reap or store away in barns, and yet your heavenly Father feeds them. Are you not more valuable than they?......see how the lilies of the field grow. They do not labour or spin. Yet I tell you that not even Solomon in all his splendour was dressed like one of these...... If this is how God clothes the grass in the field.....Will he not much more provide for you..... So do not be over worried.'* (Matthew 6 26-31)

We continued to consider how we could build bridges into our community. With so much natural beauty in flowers, fields and fauna all around, it dawned on us that we could follow our Lord's example and use it to illustrate the Christian message. Tentatively, we embarked on a flower festival with a difference. This would not be a professional promotion, but mounted with our own workforce of church members and resources. It was prompted by a desire to demonstrate God's goodness and generosity in giving us a world *'so full of splendour and of joy, beauty and light.'* For over 20 years since the festival's beginning in 1980, the texts and floral displays have combined to present many of the facets of the teachings of the Lord Jesus Christ.

For many years, a short Bible reading and a prepared prayer were included each hour on the hour throughout the festival. A variety of members took part in this brief act of worship and meditation. For many, this was their first exposure to public ministry. Several testified to the enrichment and encouragement this brought into their own lives. Others, particularly some older friends, acted as hosts, sitting and chatting to visitors in the chapel following-up thoughts from the Bible reading. Numerous people informed us of the comfort, encouragement and spiritual enrichment which resulted from those conversations. At such times, the Psalmist's words (92:13-14) seemed to resonate. '*Planted in the house of the Lord, they will flourish in the courts of our God. They will still bear fruit in old age, they will stay fresh and green.*'

Perhaps one of the greatest spin-offs from the festival was its inclusiveness. So many people of all ages were able to be physically involved and join in the ministry of the church. In 1993, there was a simple yet memorable exhibit. Jim and Marion Shakespeare, artist friends from Blackpool, painted an impressive entrance to a railway tunnel. Peering through this darkened aperture, one saw at the end an illuminated arrangement of golden freesias. Alongside this arrangement was the verse, '*God will bring me out of my darkness into the light and I will see his goodness.*' *Micah 7:9.* This Biblical text spoke graphically to many that year. We still receive comments from people who were in tunnels of grief, sadness and despair, for whom that display brought God's message of hope.

The festival always concludes with a major evening of thanksgiving entitled *Festival Praise*. So popular are these evenings that almost from their commencement they became all-ticket gatherings. New and traditional songs and hymns led by the festival choir and a small group of musicians are sung with joyful abandonment. Numerous choir contributions and solos have been memorable. John Townsend's humorous and provocative drama has caused much boisterous laughter ringing down the aisles, while, with dexterity, he infiltrates a positive truth into the minds of the audience.

Using drama in the church caused some raised eyebrows when it was first introduced. Gradually, prejudice gave place to acceptance when it was seen effectively to support our essential message. The careful use of satire and drama, which gently but purposefully deal with

83

John Townsend, chapel dramatist extraordinary.

topical issues, has often been used to effect in a Christian context.

One of John's most unforgettable sketches portrayed a negative, dour male member of a congregation. He entered dressed in a black suit with a long face, which stayed that way throughout the monologue. The theme of the festival was gratitude. The following excerpt illustrates John's talent for getting across a point to the audience. The setting is a church service.

It's the first hymn, so it's bound to be one of those praise affairs. Have you noticed how the emphasis is always on being grateful these days? Well I'm not going to sing it. After all, what have I got to be grateful for? I beg your pardon? Count my blessings! Like what?

Flowers? I can't stand the things. The pollen makes me sneeze.
Birds? They peck the blossom and ruin the washing.
Colours? I only like magnolia. I'm colour blind, anyway.
Eyes? I'm short-sighted and I'm not paying to get spectacles.
Weather? It's miserable, cold and damp and plays havoc with the arthritis.
Sunshine? It brings me out in a rash. I can't stand the heat.
Friends? I don't have any.

Food? I've got a delicate stomach, an irritable duodenum and I can't eat fish.

Family? Don't talk to me about family.

The past week? There's certainly nothing to be thankful for there – it's been dismal.

Monday *was bad:*

The budgie died in the night.

My hot water bottle went cold so I tried to reheat it in the microwave. A terrible mess.

The milkman left only semi-skimmed. That's no good on your Weetabix.

WHAT HAVE I GOT TO BE THANKFUL FOR?

Tuesday *was worse:*

It rained just when the washing was dry. The neighbour threw soot on the garden just as there was a gust of wind.

The drains got blocked and I had to phone Dynorod. They told me off for flushing the budgie down the lavatory.

WHAT HAVE I GOT TO BE THANKFUL FOR?

Wednesday *was sickening:*

I got the bill from Dynorod. A full service at the crematorium would have been cheaper.

WHAT HAVE I GOT TO BE THANKFUL FOR?

Thursday *was terrible:*

The baker left thick cut slices which are useless for the toaster. It jammed before hurling a blazing crust into the cornflakes packet which ignited and ruined the tablecloth.

WHAT HAVE I GOT TO BE THANKFUL FOR?

Friday *was abysmal:*

I went back to the doctor and told him the medicine for my athlete's foot tastes awful and is useless. He said it was ointment. He laughed at me so I'm writing to the Medical Council.

I overslept so I missed the milkman and couldn't give him a piece of my mind. He left Gold Top, which I can't stand.

WHAT HAVE I GOT TO BE THANKFUL FOR?

Saturday *was dire:*

I went to town especially to buy some eggs for the weekend, but a large lady sat on them and then had the nerve to ask for the expense of dry cleaning her camel hair coat.

WHAT HAVE I GOT TO BE THANKFUL FOR?

Sunday *I come to church and its all about being thankful! So much for praise! I wish I could put the clock back. That would show them. The more things change, the more goes down the drain, that's my saying. Oh, its time for this week's text. Just listen....it's bound to be irrelevant.*

Isaiah 43:verses 18 and 19. But the Lord says: ' Do not cling to events of the past or dwell on what happened long ago. Watch for the new thing I am going to do. It is happening already–you can see it now!'

Sometimes I wonder why I bother! Some people think you have to be praising all the time and starting new projects all over the place. Well some of us have the simple gift of sharing and talking just as I've been ENCOURAGING you. You see, some people are just not content to stay where they are – unless they've got some challenge.....some crusade with a constant smile on their face and a continual desire to change things. After all, that's got nothing to do with Christianity has it?

Pardon, (looking at an imaginary neighbour) *Is something wrong? Where are you going? Well....fancy that just walking out in the middle of a service. Was it something I said? That's the trouble here.....you can't please some people in church these days.*

Authentic drama allows us to laugh at ourselves and not at the faith we hold. It illumines and reinforces the message we preach. We can discover truth through wholesome humour. We have been fortunate to have such dedicated talent in the church family.

Alongside the numerical growth of the local church, concern for the wider world found various forms of expression. We were challenged in the 1980s by a consideration of such scriptural passages as 1 John: 17,18. *'If any one has the world's goods and sees his brother in need, yet closes his heart against him, how does God's love abide in him? Little children let us not love in word or speech but in deed and in truth.'* Here, love in action is

Sir Cliff Richard came for a weekend in 1978.

the result of two things, seeing and having. Mission, therefore, must have priority. Our large chapel has been an ideal location for evangelistic and inspirational gatherings. In the late 1970s, Sir Cliff Richard, the entertainer, shared with us a memorable weekend. Cliff and I were board members of the Evangelical Alliance Relief Fund, a major charity serving in third world countries. Over 1500 people packed the premises to hear his story of God's loving involvement in his life.

The famous Chalk Farm Salvation Army band presented a stirring weekend, and various other mission activities ensured that we were committed to sharing the good news of the Christian gospel. Our clubs for the 11-14 year age group were popular in the 1970s and 80s, with 50 to 60 young people on the register of the Inglewood club. At

Mike Cole with missionary Helen Brackenbury and church members
Tim Goulding and Cecil Pearse in Papua New Guinea 1992.

the other end of the age spectrum, Beehive, the over 60s programme,
has been well supported for many years.

Interest in world mission increased. Visiting delegations and
missionaries expanded our vision. The weekly prayer meetings were
a vital component of our mission strategy as was the monthly offering
for world needs. Michael Cole led hovercraft expeditions to Nepal and
Papua New Guinea. In recent years he has taken Gorsley friends and

others to engage in short-term building projects in the third world, and especially in Nicaragua. Under the auspices of the Peace and Hope Trust, the work parties have built classrooms, provided desks, assisted in building homes and health clinics and supported craft workers.

The church has also given considerable backing to Hazel Hendry. She was converted at a Cliff Richard evangelistic gathering in which we were involved in Gloucester. Hazel became a courageous refugee relief worker in the Balkans. In 1986, she walked the 853 miles from John O'Groats to Land's End, raising well over £20,000 in sponsorship money for TEAR Fund. For several years she collected truckloads of clothes, hospital equipment, medicines, food and furniture and took personal responsibility for delivering them to numerous relief charities in Europe. Alf and Doreen Beard continue to represent the interests of the Mission Aviation Fellowship through the west Midlands, north Wales and other parts of the country.

For many years, my wife Beryl and helpers had a regular stall in Ross-on-Wye market, trading Christian books and crafts from third world countries. This ministry expanded to include training colleges, church groups, house meetings, and displays in shop windows in Gloucester during the Easter season. At a trade exhibition on all aspects of wedding planning held in a major local hotel, Beryl noticed that there was no reference to church involvement. Mentioning this to the manager, she offered to display a white bride's Bible. Eventually, a space by the cake was offered. Within the hour she was back and the Bible was attractively displayed. When she returned to the hotel after the weekend to collect this prize exhibit, the manager apologised and said that it had been stolen. We hope that the thief found it challenging reading!

The influence of books and the church bookstall is immeasurable. One missionary medical doctor preacher, visiting Gorsley in the 1970s, declined to take a preaching fee. He asked if he could take the equivalent amount in books. Some time later he wrote, '*You may be interested to know that your giving us the book, "China, Christian students face the communist revolution," by David Adeney of the OMF, has influenced Thai government action.*

89

Beryl Goodland selling Christian literature in Ross market.

You may remember we encouraged the Thai church to translate it into their own language and have it published. The Thai government, which is now very right wing, is officially promoting its distribution to combat communism.'

The church has been deeply involved in organising the Baptist rest tent at the annual Three Counties Show in Malvern. Providing comfortable chairs, home made cakes and tea in china cups, it is a quiet haven and resting place for many weary wanderers. Information about the Christian church and a book and card stall have given opportunities to offer friendship and encouraged conversations with visitors, many of whom have very little contact with Christianity.

New approaches designed to build bridges of friendship and mutual trust in the community included numerous visiting choirs and orchestras from the USA. These outstanding groups have included the impressive Tallowood Baptist sanctuary choir from Houston, the talented handbell choir of Wilshire Baptist church, Dallas, the Sonare Orchestra from

Minnesota, Jubilation Brass, a college big brass orchestra, and visits from the male voice chorus of the Bethel college in Minnesota. We also hosted a Christian Thailand drama troupe. In a joint venture with Ross Baptist church we sponsored a young people's group from Romania, who shared a canvas camp for a week with local young people on the church playing field.

Another unforgettable evening of choral music was a visit from 30 members of the Ukrainian National Boyan Ensemble from Kiev. Delayed by bureaucracy in Moscow, the choir arrived late in England for a concert tour. On arrival they were told that all their engagements had been cancelled. The national press highlighted their plight. We learned that they were living in cramped accommodation in Malvern, stranded and without money to pay their expenses. In 48 hours we organised a concert in the chapel and provided meals. The auditorium was full and the welcome enthusiastic. The choir, accustomed to singing in grand concert halls to audiences of thousands, filled the chapel with magnificent music. At the close, the packed congregation stood and sent them on their way with a rousing rendition of *Guide me, O my great redeemer*, as a prayer for their uncertain future. The offering, expressing our Christian love and concern, raised £1,000 to help our new Ukrainian friends.

Country dinner evenings and light classical concerts with Michael Kirby, principal clarinettist with the Tenerife Symphony Orchestra, and other guests proved to be very popular. In recent years, concerts of a more populist style have resounded in the village as the chapel continues its musical tradition. Canon and Ball the comedians, and other entertainers, have been guests who have shared their personal pilgrimage into faith.

In 1985 Central Television involved the church in their *Encounter Series* of programmes. Designed to show faith in action, the film focused in on Michael Cole's role as a Squadron Leader in the R.A.F. and his responsibility for the fitness of Strike Command personnel, and my role as a rural minister to the community. It highlighted our mutual concern for people and our commitment to underprivileged communities in the third world.

From the late 1970s, the church was increasingly a venue for encouraging new life and growth in churches of our own denomination, though not exclusively. The adaptable premises and the generous hospitality and overnight accommodation offered to many visitors created a helpful setting for some outstanding consultations. In June 1989, David Coffey, now the general secretary of the Baptist Union, wrote thanking the church for hosting an interdenominational conference on evangelism. He said: '*I am convinced that when the latter part of the twentieth century Baptist life is recorded, Gorsley is sure to have its place. It has more than just good facilities. There is that special spiritual atmosphere which facilitates those who come on a conference. So many of them speak of the atmosphere of prayer and faith and vital Christianity and I hope that your folk are aware of the blessing they bring to so many others.*'

At the beginning of this period, most Baptist churches, and particularly younger ministers, could be described as evangelical. Their concerns, however, for new life, growth and renewal did not appear to be adequately reflected in meetings of the council of the Baptist Union. There was a perceived lack of concern with the spiritual and numerical decline of our churches.

A small group of ministers arranged a two-day conference in Gorsley for consideration of these issues. None of us aspired to be leaders of a new Baptist organisation. As busy ministers, we were not looking for additional burdens. We passionately desired to stimulate a movement for unity and a forum for mutual encouragement within our union. The Rev Jack Ramsbottom recorded the outcome of our 48-hour conference. (Mainstream magazine. Issue 63; September 1998). '*The inaugural meeting led to our first executive meeting at Gorsley. Ah, that name conjures-up some very happy memories – the thriving church, the lovely scenery, the marvellous meals, the warm hospitality, the genuine friendship, friendships that have stood the tests of time, and the home grown fruit and vegetables waiting to be picked up at the end of the meetings. It was at Gorsley that the name*

Lynette Goulding's scones, strawberry jam and cream are legendary.
Also pictured, L to R, Ruth Roberts, Joan Openshaw,
Sigrid Rodgers and Vena Goulding with Lynette.

Mainstream was born. It was there that Douglas McBain, in a brainstorming session, came up with the name Mainstream.'

This seminal conference led to an annual gathering in the Swanwick conference centre. This became the largest conference of Baptists outside the national annual assembly of the Baptist Union. Of the first conference, one speaker said: *'I have prayed for a people who spread such love, expectation, prayer and warmth of heart and mind and spirit, that the whole denomination is blessed…and that is what Mainstream is to be.'*

As to the wider achievements and contribution the Mainstream movement made, history will make its judgement. For Gorsley church members who offered hospitality to many visiting ministers over a 10-year period, these were days when enduring friendships were made.

We had the privilege of encouraging evangelical unity and entertaining some remarkable people.

For most of the Mainstream activities held locally, Lynette Goulding led the catering team for the main meals on the premises. Her generous helpings of home-made apple pie and custard, together with the tea-time scones with fresh cream and delicious strawberry jam, are renowned.

Gorsley also offered a venue for two-day seminars organised by Mainstream for the support and encouragement of ministers. Two, in particular, on expository preaching, led by the Rev Dick Lucas, rector of St Helen's church, Bishopsgate, London, were outstanding and over-subscribed. On one sweltering summer afternoon, over 30 of us sat in a session under a large yew tree in the spacious graveyard. Each person in turn offered his synopsis and outline of a sermon on the designated Bible passage. Imagine the conversation of two rural folk tending their relative's grave. *'What they be adoing over thar then?'* The other person who had some connection with the chapel replied, *'summit about preachin to bring people alive from the dead.'* The astounded questioner blurted, *'na you don't really mean that do ee?'* They were nearer to the truth than perhaps they were aware. The Christian message is one of new life through Jesus Christ.

Every Whitsun holiday weekend from 1977 onwards, the chapel has played host to the Royal Air Force Link-Up, a Christian fellowship for all ranks. They have come from their various stations or headquarters, with their families, their tents and caravans for three days of relaxation and fellowship. The church has often been encouraged by stories of God's enrichment of their lives and has been stimulated to pray for those who serve in our armed forces.

From the mid 1970s, our increasing congregation began to reflect a movement away from a largely agriculturist, family dominated congregation, to a more healthily balanced community. This was pleasingly representative of the changing culture in the villages. The strength of congregational government is the informed and praying church meeting. The binding cord, which keeps people with divergent opinions together, is the love and grace of God.

Considerable patience and love were required with those who were adamant that 'nothing changes here,' and the growing number of new Christians who vocally responded, 'why not?' The gospel of hope and new life in Christ is central to all our thinking and proclamation. The packaging of that unchanging good news, in terms of language and practice, will always call for re-appraisal. *'The idea of timeless English,'* wrote C.S.Lewis in one of his letters to Malcolm, *'is sheer nonsense. No living language can be timeless. You might as well ask for a motionless river.'* As with most congregations, we had to face the need for a language of worship which had no secrets. We needed deliverance from archaic phrases of heavily draperied Tudor or Victorian words and obsolete endings of the 'est' and 'eth' variety. Antiquity does not automatically convey authority, but neither can religious experience and expression always be reduced to everyday expression. Clarity of meaning there must be, but tone or sound is evocative of faith, praise and the mystery of God. The blending of divergent opinions demanded substantial pastoral involvement and an inordinate amount of calm perseverance by all involved. It is a continuing debate.

There is always a danger in rushed, superficial change, which is as pathetic as it is wearisome. Thomas Oden describes those quick solutions as *'a long parade of novelties that promise the moon and deliver green cheese. After the dust of debates and experiments is over, we are left with a church strewn with the wreckage of such fantasies.'*

First impressions are important. Villagers, visitors and 'incomers' to our village chapel need to sense a welcome and immediate acceptance. The search for security, inner peace and meaning in life sometimes prompts people to visit a church. In this rural area, we found that many who eventually became committed members were initially contacted through personal need or family crisis. Marriage, death, funerals, domestic problems, pain, illness, anxiety and the sheer pressures of life, often resulted in the first real contact with the church. The church, however, is not just an ambulance picking up life's casualties, but when people are going through these 'rites of passage' they are more open and prepared to consider deeply the purpose of life and existence.

Early one morning in 1980, a man who had lived all his life in Gorsley knocked on the manse door. I knew Albert Johnson, as I used to visit his old dad, Ossie, who had been the village blacksmith. Because he was nearly as deaf as the proverbial post and in his 90s, I used to read the scriptures and pray with him, shouting into his ear. Son Albert stood shyly in the corner of the room, observing this pastoral ministration. Father would sometimes grunt in agreement or ejaculate a loud 'amen' when familiar words 'rang a bell' with his experience, and Albert would faintly smile in appreciation.

Chapel benefactor Albert Johnson.

On this particular morning, Albert blurted out, '*Dad's dead!*'

'*Dad's dead?*' I repeated.

'*Yes, dad's dead. Early this morning,*' said Albert.

Expressing my condolence, I asked Albert whether he had a relative who could help him.

'*No.*'

'*Do you have a friend who could help you?*' I enquired.

'*No*'

'*Then would you like me to be your friend and help you?*'

'*Yes, please,*' he responded with some enthusiasm.

Over coffee, we started to sort through the paperwork, the formalities and funeral arrangements, but, more significantly, a friendship began which was to last until Albert's death in 1999.

Albert's smallholding had no running water, electricity or public utilities until 1995. He was a man of simple lifestyle and with no real formal educational achievements. He was delightfully honest, possessed a dry sense of humour, was a mine of rural knowledge and totally reliable. I learned much about rural culture from Albert. We frequently enjoyed his company over meals and regarded him as a family friend.

Perhaps our greatest joy was to see him integrated into the church family. From the Sunday following his father's death, he seldom missed an evening service. Whenever we had works days at the chapel, he was always present and active. Church members sometimes invited him to meals and many were pleased to consider him as a friend. The church enlarged his experience and appreciation of life, as we took him to Christian functions and musical performances in some of our cities. What other grouping could have embraced this lonely man and given him such broadening experiences of life? That is a part of the genius of God's church. It is inclusive and does not depend on status, gender, education or wealth for inclusion.

Nearly 20 years later, Albert left a legacy of over £60,000 to the church in his will. This is by far the greatest single gift the church has ever received. He was so grateful for the acceptance, care and support he had from the fellowship over the years and particularly during his last years as he battled with Parkinson's disease and other debilitating physical problems.

When Jesus defined his followers as *fishers of mankind*, he was being uncompromisingly frank. Fishing can be a long and sometimes tedious task requiring patience, but it can also be exciting and immensely enjoyable. One of the problems for the church ministering in an 'instant culture' is the perverse pressure to produce quick results in the short term. Often, the work of God's grace in the life of an individual is a lengthy journey into a satisfying faith. The gate into the pathway is often opened up by friendship and expressions of genuine concern and caring love.

10

SCATTERING THE SEED
FAR AND WIDE

With new activities beginning to attract new members, the need to enlarge and refurbish our premises was imperative. Little structural improvement had been attempted for 125 years, apart from the construction of the hall in 1959. By 1979, Britain was in the grip of a severe economic recession. To contemplate large expenditure seemed imprudent in the prevailing financial climate. The mood of the church meeting, however, was that a major phased extension and refurbishment plan be implemented.

Adventures in faith in difficult times call for spiritual nerve, God-given vision, believing prayer and a willingness to work. In the summer of 1979, the complete rebuilding of Suncrest, our caretaker's cottage, was commenced. Two gift days yielded over £10,000. Numerous gifts, many anonymous, flowed into the treasury during the following months, enabling us to pay every account as it was submitted. This was to be the pattern for the larger projects which followed. As a church, we were not prepared to go into debt or to mortgage our future. We affirmed the words of Hudson Taylor, the founder of the China Inland Mission, now the Overseas Missionary Fellowship, *that God's work done in God's way will never lack God's resources.*

As we contemplated the second phase, extending the hall accommodation 100% by joining the existing hall to the chapel, another of God's serendipities materialised. Some years previously, a manufacturing company had given me a large wooden hall. A

Men of the congregation laying the foundations for Inglewood hall 1977... our first building project.

London church had used this as a youth facility. The church had now completed a new permanent building. What should they do with the wooden structure which was now surplus to their requirements? We agreed to collect it.

John Cooper and friends from Stanmore Baptist church dismantled the sections. David Goulding kindly loaned a 40-feet articulated lorry, our good neighbour Gwynne Rowley drove the vehicle and a group of us enjoyed a day in north London, loading it and then bringing it back to Gorsley. It was erected by our own self-help labour and has ever since been known as the Inglewood. The extent of its usefulness became apparent when, within a few months of its siting, it served as a venue for several midweek activities during the rebuilding of the church halls. Later it became a valuable storeroom as the permanent buildings were erected. Eventually, in November 2001, it was demolished to make way for a new kitchen and enlarged hall facilities.

History was repeated in 1985. With youth work and other enterprises expanding, we were offered another solid timber building, which had been used as two school classrooms. The local education authority was now erecting a permanent building. After protracted negotiations with the contractor, it was offered to us free of charge. The only stipulation was that we had to dismantle it and move it off site in three days. Hurriedly, we called a meeting on the Wednesday evening. About 40 men and boys volunteered to take-up the challenge. During the next three days, teams worked days and into the nights, constantly refreshed by tea, coffee and snacks provided by our splendid ladies. Tractors and trailers transported loaded sections the three miles to Gorsley. The final load arrived at the chapel early on the Saturday evening. With admirable teamwork, the task had been completed with six hours to spare and not one window was broken!

George Rodgers who, in retirement, was part of a dedicated voluntary maintenance team.

The site foreman had remarked that, '*you do gooders will never do it in the time. I'll be in there on Monday morning with the bulldozer.*' He had not counted on our motivation, enthusiasm or organisation. Members of the same team who had dismantled it later erected the Park hall. Its usefulness endures.

The restoration of the extensive chapel graveyard took several years of prolonged negotiation with relatives and considerable manual work by a team of volunteers. Ant-hills, knee-high weeds, kerbstones and tumps were gradually

The exposed Gorsley stone forming an arch behind the pulpit
in the 1982 rebuilding project.

removed and headstones carefully brought into an upright position.
These improvements allowed grass cutting by volunteers using modern
machinery. Today, a well-manicured graveyard bears witness to our
respect for our forefathers.

In the summer of 1981, raging dry rot was discovered rapidly
devouring the chapel floor and sending its destructive tentacles boring
into the pews. We had no option than to engage in a major
refurbishment of our extensive premises. This was to present us with
the greatest challenge to date. The balancing of faith and responsibility
is often a delicate exercise for Christian leadership in a growth situation.
Such tension can build spiritual muscle in a prayerful, expectant
people. There were some who rightly urged great caution, while
others advised greater activity and strides of faith. This was inevitable,
yet formative. It tested the quality of our trust in, and love of, Christ
and our faith in each other. Humanly, there were times of questioning
and even doubt, but a majority sensed that God was calling us to step-
out in trust and faith.

As the contract, awarded to local builder Gerald Parker, proceeded, we were often amazed and humbled by God's provision. People came with thank-offerings, letters arrived bearing gifts from past members and new friends. *'I enclose a little gift in memory of.... She loved Gorsley Chapel, as I did too. Many thanks.'* 'I enclose £1,000 in memory of my wife for whom I thank God.' 'We were visitors to your Flower Festival. We want to make a financial covenant with the Church.' 'I was given this £5 as a present. I want to give it to Lord, as I shall spend it on myself, otherwise.' 'We have been able to sell some property. Here's a gift of £1,000 for carpeting the Chapel.' 'Here is another £34 towards the building fund. It's Christmas tips I have been given.' 'We would like to give all the steel work (£1300) for the new extensions.'* (From a young married couple.) These were typical of many letters received. Generous gifts continued to flow in each month from members and friends. As bills were presented, funds were available to meet them. A Christian business friend of mine attended a morning service in the early days of reconstruction. This was his only visit. Impressed with the spirit of worship and the warm welcome he had received, he inquired about the building programme. After lunch at the manse, he offered to match every £1 given by the church with a pound up to the sum of £10,000. *'This'* he said, *'is by way of encouragement.'* We were greatly encouraged! The Lord knew our needs and he directed his abundant supply to meet that need at a crucial time.

For all the building projects, members contributed generously, offering their talents as well as their financial resources. One young member grew cacti and the proceeds were given to the building fund. A group of members organised an auction of furniture, antiques, household goods, jewellery and a cow! Cliff Richard kindly gave us a silver disc which created some lively bidding. Over £7,000 was raised in an afternoon. Members gave over 5,000 working hours freely and joyfully to the chapel renovation programme.

The calibre of giving opened up new spiritual depths of faith. Many gave thanks to God for the opportunity to assess their possessions and declutter their lives. A young married couple gave the proceeds of a sale of wedding gifts, which they felt were surplus to their requirements. One member summed up the thoughts of many when she wrote: '*It's great to belong to such a loving family. There is such an obvious growth in the love of the folk within the body at Gorsley. I saw the Lord, high and lifted up.*' The letter contained a cheque for £2,000.

Through the autumn and cold winter of 1981-1982, volunteers laboured, removing pews, ripping-up the extensive wooden floor and filling the void where stone had been taken-out in the 1850s to build the chapel walls. A tractor-size hole was created in the side of the chapel to allow machinery access. Three hundred tons of hardcore were gobbled-up as a base was formed for the new concrete floor. An improved heating system, a larger platform area, an open baptistry and replacement windows were installed. The building was completely rewired by John Davies and Michael Harding and local helpers installed an improved public address system. Rob Davies, who grew up in the village, created and fitted a magnificent, moveable contemporary pulpit. The walls were pleasingly decorated in mist green. Dark green wall-to-wall floor carpeting gave a feel of homeliness and the comfortable wooden chairs, with golden upholstery fabric, completed the aesthetically pleasing worship centre. The approaches and frontage of the premises were re-landscaped and a new tarmacadam road was laid, giving easier access to the cemetery area, kitchen and other ancillary buildings.

One of the impressive features of the years of renovation and rebuilding was the addition of new members who possessed a variety of skills and practical abilities. Tom and Pam Hedworth, market gardeners from Kilcot, joined us in the early stages of the development programme. A family man of many skills, Tom was a down to earth person. He could be blunt and forthright when he felt the occasion required it, but he was also generous and caring. I first met him when speaking to his neighbour Peter James. Tom was polite as we were introduced, but it was obvious that he had little time for the church. Peter said to me later: '*Tom's a really good neighbour. If he became a believer, he would be a fine Christian.*'

Tom and Pam Hedworth, practical, faithful Christians.

Some time later, Tom's two daughters came to see me about arranging their weddings. They did not attend a church, but thought our building was a pleasant looking chapel for their intended ceremony.

Tom decided that he and Pam should have a look at the chapel if he was going to lead his daughters down the aisle. They attended an evening service. '*Not a bad evening, minister,*' he said, as we shook hands at the door. I suggested that I should visit them to talk over the wedding plans. They agreed. So began a pilgrimage, a dialogue and a friendship. The pilgrimage into a living personal faith in the Lord Jesus Christ, a continuing dialogue dealing with the questions arising out of their new found faith and a caring and sharing as members of the family of God.

Tom and Pam were a part of a divine provision in the renovation programme. He was a skilled builder and a man for whom high standards of craftsmanship were important. Soon after his conversion, he wanted to join in prayers at the mid-week fellowship meeting. But he had a problem, he confided. His tongue, before he became a Christian, was rather loose and expletives were a fairly common part of his vocabulary. *'What ever would the deacons say if I opened my mouth in prayer and a 'blinder' came out in my excitement?'* We agreed together to pray about the matter. Some days later, he rang me to say that at about 3 am he could not sleep. As he lay awake, he kept hearing the word *'Colossians'* buzzing in his mind. He could never recall hearing that word before. He went downstairs, picked up his Bible and searched through the index to see if this was a book in the Bible. Having discovered it was, he started reading. When he came to chapter 3 verse 8 he read: *'But now you must get rid of these things, anger, passion and hateful feelings. No insults or obscene talk must ever come from your lips.'* As he prayed over that text, he was aware of deliverance from his swearing habit. It never troubled him again. His public prayers were always memorable for their directness, practical concern and earthed spirituality. Tom never suffered fools gladly, but he was the epitome of a loving carer and someone concerned for those in need. He became a respected deacon and leader. Sadly, Tom died at a relatively young age some years later and was deeply mourned and missed by his family and the church fellowship. Pam has battled serenely with physical pain and weakness. She is living evidence of God's upholding grace and strength in the midst of weakness.

Throughout the extensive rebuilding of the premises, we did not presume on the faithfulness of God to our forefathers. We had to prove that faithfulness in the details of life for ourselves. This was exciting and spiritually uplifting. Unbelief shackles God's will and purpose; faith releases it.

The 150th church anniversary celebrated in the autumn of 1981 introduced an international dimension to the chapel fellowship. Dr

Part of the 150th church anniversary congregation.
L to R, Beryl and Pat Goodland and Lawanna and Bruce McIver from
Dallas, USA. Bruce was the guest preacher.

Bruce McIver, from Wilshire Baptist church, Dallas, Texas, was the guest preacher. Twenty-two members from his large church joined him for a week of Christian sharing and mission. Many enduring friendships sprang from that seminal week to the mutual advantage of both churches. Visitors from both congregations have sealed friendships through the years by jetting over the Atlantic. Copious communications have ensured a bond of prayer and active fellowship and have humorously confirmed that George Bernard Shaw was right—*we are two countries divided by a common language.*

An important aspect of the ministry of the church is pastoral care. We are called to bear one another's burdens and so fulfil the law of

Christ (Galatians 6:2). To befriend, support and gently advise people who appeal for help is of the essence of our faith. In the rebuilding programme of the mid-1980s, this ministry was in mind with the provision of new counselling areas, offices and the pastor's study. The disruption of domestic simplicity, dysfunctional families, homelessness, bereavement and loneliness brought an increasing number of people seeking help and support. Jackie Cole became our first part-time member of staff in 1980, as secretary and personal assistant to the minister. That appointment enabled our involvement in pastoral care to be more expansive. Jackie gave herself unstintingly to many aspects of the ongoing ministry of the church. The old vestry became her office, while I was housed in a renovated stable. New modern offices were built in 1984. Manual typewriters gave place to electric models, which today have rightly been replaced by more adept computers.

The genius of the Christian church is that it is a collection of people who admit their failures and, through faith in the Lord Jesus, receive forgiveness, acceptance, love and inner strength from God. Christians are always in the process of 'becoming.' The Church therefore is a community of 'roots and fruits.' The New Testament speaks of being rooted in Christ. The church, which will be vital in its life and fruitful in its community, will give evidence of the fruit of compassionate love, joy and a sense of peace. This will surmount the clash between the generations, special interest groups and diverse social backgrounds. The biggest barriers to developing a living church are unfounded fears, self-preoccupation, guilt, jealousies and a sense of inferiority.

In the ideal kingdom of God, we are colour blind and class blind. We see in each other a person who is precious to God and for whom Christ cares. Though this compelling attitude has never been achieved fully in the history of this rural church, it has been a goal and has resulted in some splendid corporate and individual caring ministries. A church is always at its best and most effective when Christ's love inspires its distinctive lifestyle and motivates its commitment to the local community and to the larger world.

Violet Holland, whose lifestyle was transformed through Christian friendship.

'*Evicted woman makes roadside home in tent,*' screamed the newspaper headline. Deacon Gordon Bright was soon on the phone from Kempley where the drama was unfolding. Television cameras were on site when Gordon and I arrived. Violet had cared for her invalid parents in their small bungalow for years. They had both died without leaving a written will, but verbally promising the home to their single and caring daughter. Her brothers wanted to sell the property and obtained an eviction order. The bailiffs enforced the court decision and Violet was left stranded in the bitterly cold conditions of March 1985. That's how we found her, with her few possessions in a zinc bath tub and her growling large German shepherd dog, sitting on the grassy verge outside her former home.

She was adamant that she had no intention of leaving the village. Some church members loaned a tent, others provided hot meals and we continued to negotiate. On the fourth day of her protest, as snow covered the tent and grass verge, Violet agreed to occupy a caravan which we had found nearby. Carrying her earthly possessions up the incline into her temporary home, I noticed she was wheezing and breathless. Within weeks, doctors confirmed she was suffering with cancer. By this time she was re-housed in our chapel bungalow complex. Several members of the church shared the responsibility of ferrying her to hospital, befriending and caring for her. Gradually, this young woman from gypsy stock, who could neither read nor write, relaxed, found friendship and a faith in a loving God. Baptised at her request on 3rd August 1986, she became integrated into the church family. With growing confidence she took part in activities and contributed her practical skills. On the last Sunday evening service of the year, it was our practice to have a time of sharing, when individuals could come forward to the microphone and share testimonies of God's goodness in their lives. The congregation was greatly surprised and delighted when Violet strode quickly down the aisle and into the pulpit. There was hardly a dry eye in the large congregation as she recounted the joy she had experienced in her new found faith and thanked the church for their kindness. We witnessed a miracle that evening. Violet, who usually had little conversation, spoke for about five minutes. As some friends commented, '*It was as though she had the gift of tongues!*' Her long battle with cancer ended peacefully during the 1988 flower festival. She died having been nursed and lovingly supported by her Christian family. Providentially, our daughter Hilary, a trained nurse, was living in Gorsley for 12 months. Each evening for the last six months of Violet's life, she was able to attend to her needs and give her professional support.

Through the years, several young people have been called to serve the wider church and international communities. As mentioned earlier, Dora Cracknell went to China, Pearl Griffiths served in Nepal and India. Leslie Beard and Tony Aubrey became Baptist pastors in England. Nick Cole is communications manager with the Redcliffe Christian college, while his sister Carolyn serves with Youth with a Mission, teaching students from third world countries English and cultural studies.

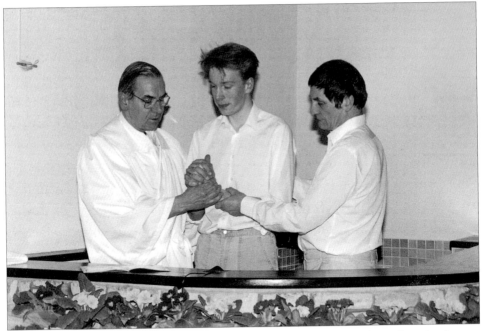

One of the many baptisms by full immersion which have taken place in the chapel. L toR: Pat Goodland (pastor), Rob Goulding (candidate), Bill Openshaw (deacon).

Robert Goulding is in training for leadership with the New Frontiers church in Winchester, and Kathy Barlow has recently taught English language in Thailand for a year in a mission environment.

Lilian James is a much travelled member of the congregation. She has taught in Tewkesbury, New Zealand, Qatar in the Arabian Gulf, Nigeria and Malaysia. A peripatetic teacher of deaf and partially hearing children, she still responds enthusiastically to calls for supply teaching. Evangeline Goulding, after teaching for a number of years in London, set sail for the Seychelles. For 17 years, she taught sailing and developed water sports for the island's young people. Many of her young proteges have taken part in international competitions.

From its earliest beginnings, the church has been convinced that education is an integral part of Christian commitment to the community. John Hall initiated the first library in the village and was himself the headteacher at Gorsley Goffs for 25 years in the 19th century.

Numerous members have served on the school governors' board, representing either the Goff Trust or the local education authority. They include Gerald Adams, Elizabeth Bishop, Doreen Beard, R.C.Goulding, Julian Goulding, Lilian James, Alf Watkins and myself. In addition, Alf Watkins, Gerald Adams and I had the privilege of being chairman of the board at various times. The present headteacher, Clive Westall, and his family are members of the chapel. The spacious chapel auditorium has been used by the school for various community events. These included the 175th school anniversary service, and a major production (1994) of '*The man who made a million and gave it all away*,' a drama telling the rags-to-riches story of the school's benefactor, Edward Goff. On another occasion, more than 700 people – including some of the original evacuees from Birmingham— attended two performances of a major musical '*Strangers in the countryside.*' This extravaganza depicted the invasion of evacuees from Birmingham and Liverpool at the beginning of World War II. This proved to be a hands-on means of teaching history.

The erection of six senior citizens' bungalows on church land was another expression of care for vulnerable people. The first three were opened in 1983 and the second phase was completed in 1988. Arthur Jones gave incentive for this project. A long-time deacon who had become elderly and infirm, he lived alone in a cottage in Kempley. He felt vulnerable and isolated. Valuing his independence, he did not want to become a resident in a town nursing home. He wished to remain in the familiar rural area in which he had lived for so many years. Following a heart attack, he came to the manse for a period of recovery. In conversation, he expressed a wish to live near the chapel. '*Pastor, can't you do something? The church has been my life and now I'm old I don't want to leave it.*' The challenges of such sentiments, with their implicit strong hint that we should take some responsibility for an ageing population, resulted eventually in our modest wardened accommodation complex. Arthur was our first resident. He was constantly expressing gratitude for his 'chapel bungalow.' The closing months of his life were

Chapel bungalows. The chapel management committee arranges all maintenance so that residents are freed from a whole range of concerns.

surrounded by love and tender care from his many chapel friends and his family.

Les Aubrey has recently returned to Gorsley and happily occupies one of the bungalows. Having lost his wife Sylvia, and being unable through incapacity to tend his garden in his former home in Ross, he now enjoys being back in the village. He was born and bred here and lived for most of his life in the Old Post Office. His supportive family live close by, which is an added bonus. Mr Aubrey is delighted to be 'local' again. The church is equally thrilled to have this link with a family that has been associated with the chapel for 200 years.

Anne Sherwin became the chapel caretaker in 1972. She came from the notorious Moss Side district of Manchester and the sprawling Wythenshawe council estate. She escaped from a tragic domestic trauma and found refuge in rural Herefordshire. Church at that time found no place on her personal agenda, but the offer of a job with tied housing was appealing. Anne didn't attend the services for three years, knowing little about Christianity and caring even less. Then Anne hesitantly

The indefatigable Anne Sherwin.

attended her first Sunday evening service. The sermon was based on Paul's writings in Ephesians 5:14, '*Awake you that sleep, arise from the dead, and Christ shall give you light.*' The scripture was eventually to prove prophetic in a very real way, though almost certainly not in the way the writer Paul meant.

Anne's attendance at church increased. On Monday evenings, one of its members, Ann Goulding, always called on Anne for a chat. During one of those regular Monday evening social occasions, I joined in. She says: '*That night I went to bed, but I tossed and turned and couldn't sleep a wink. I firmly believe God was speaking to me and challenging me to give my life to Him and let Him walk alongside me for the rest of my days. So at 2 a.m. I said, "Right Lord. If you want me you can have me." I just committed my life to Him and the moment I did so I felt a beautiful peace and the room actually glowed. With my northern working class roots, I am a realist. I am not prone to fantasies. I was so sceptical that I got out of bed and went to the window to see if there were car headlights in the lane. There was nothing. It was then that I remembered the first text I had heard read at a Gorsley Sunday service...and Christ shall give you light. A few days later I expressed my new found faith publicly in the waters of baptism. I used to be a real good time girl, drinking and smoking 40 cigarettes a day and swearing. All that is gone. I still love a good time, but today that means sharing my life with God and the people at the chapel who, like a loving family, have supported me through thick and thin.'*

Since that life-changing week in 1978, Anne has suffered from cancer on two different occasions and in two different places in her body. Both times she has known a measure of healing....she believes by the power of God.

For 26 years and through all the major dusty renovations of the premises, she kept the chapel buildings looking like a new pin! Anne also became the warden of the bungalow project, combining the post with her duties as caretaker of the chapel until her retirement in 1999. She now lives in one of the chapel bungalows she so efficiently wardened. Joanne Parsons is the new warden and chapel caretaker.

Another unforeseen avenue for service opened in the early 1980s. In an annual report, mention is made of 25 groups visiting the church for home-made teas. All groups are made most welcome. For a number of years, Vena Goulding and Pam Howley headed up this important ministry of hospitality. With their inventive team of home-made cake-makers, these teas were much in demand by sightseeing tourist groups. When they retired, Sally Adams took on the role of welcoming hostess. A well-stocked bookshop and card display dispense good literature on every occasion the chapel premises are in use. Community lunches, the Beehive (a group for the over 60s), keep-fit classes, mums and toddlers groups and the festival choir continue to have their place in the weekly schedule of this caring community. Youth groups enjoy a wide variety of activities regularly, while a range of Bible study cells find a prominent place in the church's calendar.

In his annual report to the church meeting in February 1985, the church secretary, Keith Goulding, concluded his speech with these words: '*We are in momentous days and if the opportunities given are not taken, they may be lost for ever, but if grasped Christ's kingdom will be seen in Gorsley.*' Thankfully, the chapel congregation continued to grasp, in part, further opportunities for service and ministry.

The year 1989 was eventful by any measurable standard. Dudley Callison, from Texas, joined us as an assistant, with special responsibility for young people. This was an experiment that led to the appointment of Keith Knapton as associate pastor. He served for three years before moving into another pastorate. The month of May saw the invasion of 50 young people from Baylor university, Texas. They joined a similar number of local young people from the Ross Baptist church and our own in a major outreach entitled Christian Awareness Week. Louie Giglio, from Baylor, a gifted youth communicator, was the main speaker. A large choir, uniformly clad in white T-shirts, each with a *Crossroads* logo prominently visible, sang magnificently under the direction of Tom Mosley, from Houston, Texas. The team shared their personal faith in large school assemblies, classroom encounters, on the streets of Ross and in a series of evening rallies. A public relations person was goggle-eyed as he witnessed hundreds of young people disgorging from the chapel each evening, chattering with the youthful *Crossroads* team. '*It's a bit like Pentecost!*' he exclaimed.

It was not an easy mission because 90% of the teenagers had probably never been to a Sunday school or entered the door of a church building. Many had questions which they wanted to explore, such as: '*Where do we get our values?*' '*What's wrong with promiscuous sex?*' '*Why don't our parents bother about preserving the world instead of polluting it?*' '*What's wrong with recreational drugs?*' Not all the enquirers or interested participants went on to be distinctive Christians. Some have, but others were made aware of the Christian message. Seed was sown and will eventually bear fruit. As one young graduate, among others, witnessed: '*I came broken and weary, but even the thick walls of the chapel seemed to be oozing love.*'

The 1989 united mission to youth 'Christian Awareness Week'
with the Crossroads choir.

1989 saw the acquisition of Hillview, an adjoining property to the rear of the chapel. This became the residence of our associate youth pastor and enabled the chapel to enlarge the car park. Alf Watkins, Alan Whitfield, Reg Crane, George Rodgers and Roy Millington took responsibility for this new property, transforming it into a very habitable home.

Beryl and I retired in September 1994, conscious of our own limitations and failings, but rejoicing in God's faithfulness. The following year the church secretary, in his 'state of the church' report, was able to say: '*The retirement of Pat Goodland as pastor was the end of an era. History will record that the 18-year pastorate was a successful one. Most noticeable has been an 80% increase in membership during that time and the providing of the extra facilities which are now in constant use.'*

During the interregnum, Charles Crosland, minister of Ross Baptist church, became the moderator. The deacons and the church were very grateful for his gracious and wise leadership. The superintendent of the West Midlands Baptist Association, the Rev Brian Nicholls, gave helpful support. He was able to comment that during the two-year period between ministers, the health of the church was excellent. His stated appraisal was: *'(1) The chapel has the largest evening congregation in the West Midlands. (2) The people love their Bibles. (3) The congregation includes a good number of young people.'*

11

NEW BUDS, NEW BLOSSOM

A new era began with the arrival of the Rev John Lewis and his family. The induction was held on 2nd November 1996. A large welcoming congregation assured the new minister of their commitment and support. During the interregnum, Hillview cottage had been remodelled into a spacious new manse, with double garage and all modern conveniences.

New leaders ignite new initiatives. The annual flower festival has been extended to what is now known as the Wye Valley Christian Festival. Large marquees are now a feature of the landscape during the August Bank Holiday weekend. Bible ministry is given each morning in the main marquee and celebrity speakers share their stories at inspirational evening gatherings. A children's programme swings into

Rev John Lewis (1996-)

action each day, while teenagers have their Christian pop music and talk session on Friday evening.

A new logo has been adopted, *A country church with a heart for the country* denoting the church's commitment to mission. On alternate Wednesday evenings the chapel is a hive of industry. Under the title PGI (Praise God it's Wednesday) a mid-week programme for the family has been developed. Following an early evening meal, a variety of Christian educational and devotional programmes are on offer. The choice includes the Alpha introductory course to Christianity. This international syllabus has attracted wide media attention. David Suchet, the popular actor, says: *'I cannot think of any course that covers the introduction of core beliefs of the Christian faith in such an accessible way and is so relevant for today.'* Numerous new members have been brought into the fellowship of the church through this initiative.

Other courses include a growth course in practical Christian living, and a Network series, with its emphasis on Christian servanthood. Spirituality, a contemporary buzz word in common parlance with a variety of other world faiths, is examined on another course aimed at developing a Christian prayer life and a more meditative walk with God. The diet at PGI is varied and wide-ranging. There is no need for any member to be ignorant of the basic faith of Christianity and its practice.

A recently issued paper entitled *Visions and Values* seeks to define the current aims of Gorsley Baptist church. These are expressed under five headings, Exaltation, Evangelism, Establishment, Equipping and Enabling, and Encouragement. In summary these are spelt out as:

1. **Exaltation.** This embraces all that leads people to worship God. *'Our worship seeks to bring together the best of different styles, with a real desire to help people draw near to God and know the reality of his presence.'*

2. **Evangelism.** The aim is to encourage all members to establish relationships with the unchurched. *'To help people who are saying 'no' to God to say 'yes'.'*

3. **Establishment.** Through Bible teaching, house groups and providing opportunities for worship, prayer and discussion to build relationships.

4. **Equipping and Enabling.** This goal expresses the desire of the fellowship to grow in Christian maturity. To provide assessment and

evaluation of members' spiritual gifts and to help them use them more effectively.

5. **Encouragement.** Words and deeds of encouragement build people and aid the development of character. Words of appreciation and letters of thanks stimulate people to greater achievement. The vision is to create a more positive people.

These are the stated goals and values expected of members. They are laudable, but only possible where the grace of God is active, bringing flexibility and significant valuing of each member in the fellowship.

The church is supportive of a number of missionary enterprises. Locally, it engages in several outreach activities sharing God's good news of Jesus Christ, who can meet the spiritual hunger that so many feel. Country dinner evenings, at which popular Christian entertainers and celebrities speak of their work and faith, holiday clubs for children, a massive 5th November village bonfire celebration and a full Christmas programme are all held to spread the good news.

Kempley Sunday school is an enduring feature of Christian community dedication. The work was closed during World War ll, in this village chapel three miles from Gorsley. The Rev Stapleton reopened it in the 1950s. When he left for Australia, he handed over responsibility to Janet Forty. She had just returned to her home village from college, having qualified as a day school teacher. Janet later married Keith Gooch and together with Helen Taylor (nee Forty) they have led this imaginative programme with a freshness which is totally commendable. For their Christmas carol service in December 2001, the building overflowed with probably the largest congregation ever seen on these premises.

The church in Gorsley has encouraged missions from its earliest days. It adopted a new policy document on commitment to world outreach in the winter of 2001. Its slogan for the uncharted new century is '*A country church with a heart for the whole world.*' In this lengthy document, the world outreach team, formerly the missions committee, has stated its objective, and calls for a more robust approach to mission. *'The world outreach team will develop and co-ordinate a dynamic mission involvement that will significantly impact every area of church life and seek to involve in a positive and encouraging way every member and person who attends activities at Gorsley Baptist church. The team will seek to integrate world outreach programmes with local outreach activities of the church.'*

Ed Taylor, who was brought to church by his parents Joe and Helen, has been a member of the congregation since his birth. He is an exemplar of the church's teaching and commitment through the years. Having completed his university studies with distinction, he set off in the summer of 2001 for Albania. Joining a Christian witness team, they sought through drama, music and speaking through interpreters, to proclaim the message of Jesus. The gospel of hope and reconciliation is never more needed than today in this formerly oppressed country. Ed said, *'The whole experience was brilliant. The hospitality was great. We met many challenging situations. It was the most rewarding experience of my life. I'm going back next summer.'*

The church in Britain is awash with papers, mission conferences and mission statements. People like Ed, and dozens of other members of the chapel, have gone out in teams on short and long-term mission enterprises. They earth and embody the hopes of such policy documents and give substance to the high hopes for greater involvement.

The church continues to encourage Mainstream activities. It is part of a re-focused 'word and spirit network,' which promotes regional conferences that bring together church leaders for prayer, encouragement and support in ministry and mission. The expressed purpose is to forge together a strong community of churches committed both to the word and spirit, sharing common values and a common vision for the church. Several days each year, large groups of ministers and leaders converge on Gorsley from the Midlands and Wales. Inspirational speakers share their wisdom and understanding of God's movements in the contemporary world. Discussions, sharing in prayer and in meals, bring their own encouragement to busy and sometimes dispirited leaders.

Line drawing of the new Haven family centre 2002. (Sam Eedle)

The new £160,000 Haven family centre, consisting of a series of fully-carpeted and comfortably furnished rooms, is used mainly for the growing number of children. Special guests Eddie and Nora Stobart opened the centre in the millennial year. Committed Christians for over fifty years, Eddie, whose name appears on the massive fleet of haulage lorries which are a familiar sight on the motorway network, said in his address: '*What has been achieved at this church since it was established 170 years ago has been done step by step. This is just another step in the work that goes on until Jesus comes again.*' Church organisations such as Acorn, activities for mums and toddlers, A-Zone, children's and young people's Sunday groups and mid-week adult Bible study cells use the centre regularly. Community groups use this pleasantly appointed new centre. The Salter's Hill Trust, a charity for young adults with learning difficulties, use it for art classes and occasional staff training sessions. *Teens in Crisis*, an organisation engaged in school ministries, also occupy the Haven one evening each week as a counselling centre. Church member Nathan Jones leads this needful ministry in this dysfunctional and frayed family era.

A youth group appreciating the new facilities of the Haven centre

To build the Haven, as well as direct and covenanted giving, a whole range of fund raising activities and initiatives were undertaken by industrious members. Coffee mornings, golf tournaments, sponsorships and a mammoth promise auction were among the whole raft of inventive ideas listed. The pastor offered to cook meals in people's own homes for a reasonable hourly rate. The takers were surely being asked to take steps of faith in such a deal! We understand the meals were scrumptious and the clients suffered no ill effects. Did his wife Mandy, who is a superb cordon bleu cook, coach pastor John? Bird-watching expeditions, car journeys and hours of house cleaning were also on offer. Perhaps Bruce Gilbert undertook one of the most strenuous activities. He joined the Andes Challenge, a charity fundraising enterprise, to climb the 6,000 metre Mount Cotopaxi, Equador- the highest active volcano in the world. Bruce raised £1,900 for the Haven project.

David John, the current church secretary, in thanking many people who had given their manual skills, time and money for the successful building and completion of phase one of the chapel's current project, was able to announce that *'the bills for this new extension have all been paid.'* Phase two began in the autumn of 2001. In exceptional dry and sunny conditions, numerous members of the church, under the watchful eye of David Clark and Ian Parsons acting as voluntary agents, demolished the old wooden Inglewood hall and excavated and heaped tons of earth and concrete. This assignment has increased the main hall capacity 100% and provided an enlarged modern kitchen.

In the autumn of 2001, the church welcomed a new youth minister whose major responsibility will be the many-faceted children's and young people's programme. Jon Hills, a member of Southborough Baptist church, Bromley, joined a Baptist Missionary Society 'action team' and served for six months in Zimbabwe. He trained for ministry at Spurgeon's college. His wife Susan is a schoolteacher.

Elizabeth Bishop has served the church in a fulltime capacity for nine years as church administrator and youth co-ordinator. She is deeply appreciated. Liz is a local lady who as a child attended our Sunday school and youth fellowship. Following graduation from university, she joined the church staff in 1992.

The chapel, along with numerous other churches in the United Kingdom, has an Internet web site (www.gorsleychapel.co.uk). By using this technology, surfers can now gain information about church activities and download audio sermons.

A Mori poll commissioned by Nestles in the millennial year showed the church in England to be *'one of the least respected institutions in Britain.'* In the 21st-century, churches are entities in transition. It is the speed of change which can be seen as threatening. Our post-modern and post-Christian culture is very individualist. It is predominantly a 'me culture' which says, in effect, that there is no truth except the truth as I see it. But this is also an insecure society. The basic human need for relationships, a sense of belonging and a purpose and

The minister and deacons 2002.
Back row L to R: Gordon Gilbert, Richard Jones, David John (secretary),
Steve Booth (treasurer), Ian Brown, Wilf Goulding, Ted Kania.
Front row: Jeff Goulding, Derek Wadley, Sue Upward, Sylvia Goulding,
Liz Bishop (church administrator), Keith Gooch.
Kneeling: Jon Hills (youth minister) John Lewis (pastor).

meaning in life remains unfulfilled. Within the Christian church, these longings can be met in Christ and through his people. Christianity is about feelings and emotions, but it is also deeply committed to using the mind, setting our minds on truth and grappling with it until it makes sense, giving direction and meaning for life.

12

PROMISES OF LIFE TO COME

Where does the church feature in the third millenium? For numerous secular commentators, the Christian church is already a corpse awaiting final burial. No one disputes that these are unsettling times for the church. Despite some notable exceptions, Christianity is not flourishing in the United Kingdom. Considerable examination of what has been familiar in terms of belief and practice is taking place. The smouldering older culture, with its Christian undertones, is being smothered and subdued in the jungle of rapid change. Past certainties are being challenged and past securities dented.

Dr Nigel G Wright, principal of Spurgeon's College, London, comments: *'The future of the church, as with every other part of life, is going to be more diverse and complex than ever we have known. Within this future, it is crucial to maintain the tension of stability and adventurousness. One without the other would amount either to tedious stodginess or ephemeral volatility.'* (*Mainstream Magazine*, autumn 2001).

It is suggested that *'the church is only one generation away from extinction.'* Such a thought could paralyse us into inaction if the church is only a human institution, but God is in a dynamic relationship with his church and with the world. He is always breaking out of the boundaries and limitations we impose upon him, and shattering our despairing predictions.

Soon after arriving in Gorsley, I became officiating chaplain to Royal Air Force, Hereford. It was a training centre at that time. For an hour a week for the first six weeks of their training, the young men and women at the centre attended a padre's hour. I made it clear from the outset of any sessions I led that nothing they said would be documented or reported. They needed to know, also, that they were not there for the compulsory hour to listen to some spouting 'sky pilot padre' groaning on incessantly. They were expected to join in the 'no holds barred' discussion and they often did with some ferocity.

I learned a great deal about some of their ideas and misconceptions of Christian morality, the church and the word 'love.' Few had been in a church, so their views were not shaped by personal experience. The popular media had conditioned their thinking. For instance, they could not comprehend why church dignitaries dressed up in long dresses in church and yet wanted to be called 'father.' Many of their assumptions were contrived and unfounded. The majority of these fine young people viewed the church as archaic and irrelevant in a post-modern culture. I was only too willing to agree with some of their half-truths. These were lively, enjoyable and challenging encounters for the padre! I heard despairing notes about the future of the world. With H.G.Wells, it was often suggested that the human species was doomed to be destroyed by its own stupidity. Their reactionary thinking was frequently: *let's eat, drink and be merry, for tomorrow..... well who knows? We may not be around tomorrow.* Shallow optimism or quick-fix religious wordplay has never been an option for defenders of the Christian faith. These intelligent recruits would not buy sentimental religious speak.

Though the church was 'off limits' as a topic of interest, there was a sneaking regard for the Jesus of the gospels. His reactionary character, his short shrift with fake religion, and the courageous faith that led him to an early death, brought flickers of positive response. They could relate to this unstuffy young man who could associate with the rich and poor, the healthy and sick. This was the stuff of the real world. The history of the church is not always a compelling thing; it has been a mixture of the sordid and the sublime. Jesus, however, is still good news.

The dangers in a crisis are knee-jerk reactions. We can sometimes take subtle pleasure in finding scapegoats on whom we can load blame.

It would be audacious in this limited space even to try to examine in any detail the possible reasons for the declining attendance at churches in Great Britain. The influence of the media, however, must feature on any agenda when considering the church's demise, particularly the conspiracy of the so-called secular intelligentsia. Christianity and religion often get a raw deal from media moguls. Respected atheist or agnostic scholars, who are sticklers for accuracy in their own disciplines, are wheeled-out to pontificate on faith and religion. They often do so with bewildering inaccuracy. They are partners with those who disparage religion in general and Christianity in particular. Often, their approach is that modern philosophy and people of intellect have outgrown the superstitions of religion. The assumption is that you are a little weak in your mind and odd if you believe in God.

The late John Harriott in the *Tablet* (13 October 1990) exposed this position with commendable clarity when he argued that, '*strangest of all is the curious assumption that to close the door on religion is to step into a wider world. Argue by all means that the believer's universe is a delusion, but not that a vision of human life, stretching beyond time and space, is smaller than one that sees it ending in a handful of dust...and that to believe, human beings are infinitely precious to God, reflecting his nature which they are born to share, and by grace can stretch their powers beyond their natural reach, is somehow less enriching and enlarging than to think them just animal slime. Delusion it may be, but at least a dynamic delusion, adding point and energy and nobility to life. To reject it, if rejected it must be, is hardly a matter for self-congratulation, but rather for mourning and the drawing-down of blinds.*'

Without wanting to overstate the case, there are many eminent people occupying university chairs, military leaders, politicians and men and women of erudition, who believe in God and are sympathetic to traditional Christian beliefs and values.

Living in a society in which a huge majority of citizens seldom consider the church, what hope is there of a spiritual renaissance? The search after something larger is one of the more obvious and hopeful characteristics of human nature. Some search in the area of politics for justice and understanding. Others seek for the next 'buzz,' sexual deviation, drug or hedonistic experience. Many would acknowledge a need for meaning to life. The ultimate enemy of contemporary culture is not pain, disease, poverty or evil. It is the sense that life is going nowhere. The impression that life is meaningless leads to feelings of being superfluous, unwanted and unloved. This can funnel people into a pit of sheer despair and destruction.

The Christian message is one of hope and fulfilment. It also speaks of things yet to be made known. There are times in life when we can encounter mysterious beauty in nature or in the sheer goodness of people's actions. These experiences are incoherent, but unmistakable, and are often lost in the welter of materialistic living.

I recall many years ago being called to comfort a wealthy man. He had been in the loft of his large house, fallen through the ceiling, broken his two legs and was now confined to a hospital bed where he had little control over his circumstances. He was furious. His behaviour toward the nursing staff was bossy and obnoxious. '*Padre,*' said the ward sister, '*his behaviour is intolerable. Do you think you could talk to him and perhaps calm him?*' Several weeks later, and after numerous conversations, he spoke to me about his long life. His goal had been to be materially wealthy. In that pursuit he had been ruthless. Now he confessed in words like these: '*I am beginning to see that I have missed out on so much which this life can offer. I now see beauty in nature, in colour and in the early morning sunrise. I sense a growing appreciation for other people. I had grown insensitive to any spiritual feelings. Padre, I don't know if you can understand this, but in a strange way I am grateful for the accident.*' He was beginning to see that the mystery of life becomes intelligible through the person and teaching of Jesus, who claims to be one with God.

Many who have deserted the church have not necessarily lost a personal faith in a living God, but are discontented and bored by what the church is offering. In a materialistic and mechanical world, people are struggling to maintain an active faith. People require support in times of need and to be reassured in times of doubt. There are also problems endemic in a pressurised society. Increasingly, the demands of busy lives and hectic schedules, together with the expectations of family, leave people exhausted at the weekend.

It would be pretentious and impertinent to suggest that there is a simple formula to bridge the gap between the believer and the non-believer. It would be audacious even to think that Gorsley Baptist church has always been a successful congregation and can offer some special prescription for church growth. Providence has not shone upon us in some exceptional and mysterious way, for God does not breed or encourage spoilt children. But are there elements in our story which have stood the test of time and point forward, through the mists of bewilderment, to a continuing church in the third millennium?

Evidence seems to be surfacing, and history confirms the teaching of scripture, that a church can grow healthily if it is prepared to take the words and teaching of Jesus Christ seriously. To do so is to follow Jesus and to get involved in what he is doing in the world. He came to a world which had been created perfect, but which has been besmirched by the selfishness and pride of mankind.

The primary purpose of the church is to be an agent of God's continuing programme to redeem the world through Jesus, and to restore what selfish sinfulness has scarred and wrecked. God calls his people to use their gifts to build a community that reaches out to a world in need of restoration. We are workers together with God to free creation, *'which is groaning and longing to be set free from the bondage of sin.' (Romans 8)*. The church is to be a generating powerhouse of loving support, encouragement and teaching. The church must also be outward looking, serving compassionately and modelling unity within the local community.

God always seems to reveal himself in the ordinary ways of life. We must find him in the everyday events of daily living. John Hall, in the early 19th century, found that to be true in this rural outback as he became involved with the local community, and so must we. God is not remote, but involved in the world of his creation. The church, ideally, is to be the instrument for revealing the love and concern of God and being a signpost directing attention to the saviour of the world.

In our matter-of-fact world, people demand to see the difference a living faith makes in a believer's life. *'Don't tell me, show me,'* is the new millennium slogan. When the church is seen through its members to be following Christ and living in the strength of his spirit, there is a reaction. The Royal Air Force recruits would talk about Jesus because he was not slated as the chief executive of some gigantic ecclesiastical corporation. He was worth considering because he had time for all kinds of people, for the wealthy and the deprived, for publicans and sinners and for the healthy and the suffering of this world.

The world is increasingly dismissive of male-dominated organisations and distrustful of denominational dogmatism. Too often, the church in the west has projected an image of power, prestige, jealousies, petty ego building and personal jostling for position. There is need for repentance and prayer that the church may be delivered from such pretentious pomposity. The church of the 21st century will need to be seen as more accepting and non-judgemental of those, who, in a dysfunctional world, have lost their moral bearings. This is the era of mobility, divorce, blended families, broken relationships and individual isolation. The older social fabric is severely frayed. There is a need to make concessions to human fallibility and moral failure, while emphasising the possibility of gracious reform and spiritual growth. In upholding Christ's ideals, the church must not condemn itself by hardness of heart. *'Whichever of you has committed no sin may throw the first stone.' John 8:7*. To achieve this frame of mind, teaching and preaching will have high priority.

Perhaps the most exciting feature at the beginning of the new millennium is the rapid international growth of the Christian church. In the Western world it is in demise numerically, but throughout the world 70-75,000 people daily are making their confession for the first time that *Jesus Christ is Lord*.

Two thousand years ago Jesus proclaimed in the little buffer state of Palestine, '*I will build my church and the gates of hell will not topple it over.*' At the gates of any small town in those parts would be found a group of wise men. It was there that counsel was taken and decisions made, a place of political power. What Jesus is saying is that whatever men say, whatever shade of political opinion may temporarily be dominant, no earthly power or unseen evil will be able to ultimately frustrate the building of Christ's kingdom.

For 2,000 years, forces have ranged themselves against Christ's church, from the ferocious Roman Emperors such as Nero or Flavius Domitian, to modern day communists and materialistic secularists. The oppressors have come and gone, but the church marches on. The local church is a partial expression of Christ's universal church. It has sometimes marched along its pilgrim way joyfully and enthusiastically. At other times, like wounded warriors, it has limped, faltered and fallen. This local church has known days of great happiness and times of deep sorrow during the years of its history. By the grace of God, the church is alive today with hope, rejoicing in the love and goodness of God and his redeeming faithfulness.

The church of living people, who know God through Jesus Christ, is here to stay. They have found that living daily in the company of God brings wholeness, fulfilment and lasting meaning. The way forward lies in awareness that human nature is flawed yet forgivable, and in believing passionately that God will continue to shape and nurture our lives. The future church will need to continue the process of examining its weaknesses and strengths, to reach out in relationship to others and break down cultural barriers. Communication to our local and wider communities is essential. It is dependent on integrity, honesty, openness and involvement. For two millennia, Jesus Christ has inspired adoration, worship, wonder, holiness, healing, education, abolition of slavery, resistance to injustice and evil, courage, sacrifice, art and love. He will continue this process, and we are confident that even 'the gates of hell' will not prevail against him and his kingdom. We are ultimate optimists, for we are in the hands of a cosmic God.

The Gorsley Baptist chapel has been a landmark in the village for nearly 150 years. However, it is only a building. The real church consists of people who have been worshipping God in this area for over 200 years. As a part of the world-wide Christian church, members are committed to Christ, to one another and to the service of God in the world. This includes proclaiming the word of God, prayer, evangelism, social action and the promotion of justice, education and peace. Insofar as the church is loyal to such a ministry, she will always be making constructive history in the community and in the wider world.

READING AND SOURCES

David Cox   *Personal Memoirs* (5 volumes)

David L Edwards   *From the 18th Century to the First World War.*
                     (Collins)

Patrick J Goodland   *The Flame of Faith.* (Out of print)

Richard Harries   *Questioning Belief.* (SPCK)

Christopher Hibbert *Charles 1.* (Penguin)

M E Hobbs   *Gorsley Baptist Chapel. (1852-1952)*
                     Centenary booklet

Simon Jones   *Why bother with the church?* (IVP)

J H Lloyd   *The life of Edward Goff.*
                     (Pilley Collection, Hereford Library)

Ernest A Payne   *The Story of the Baptists.*
                     (Baptist Union Publications)

J C Shambrook   *Life of John Hall.* (Out of print)

John Stott   *The Incomparable Christ.* (IVP)

Dave Tomlinson   *The Post evangelicals.* (Triangle)

Gorsley Baptist church minute books 1831-2000.

Journals, miscellaneous papers, newspaper articles, and personal interviews.

EXTENSION AND RENOVATION PROGRAMME 1977–2001

1977	Inglewood hall transported and erected.
1980	Caretaker's cottage enlarged and restored.
1980	Church hall extended by joining chapel to existing hall.
1980-1987	Chapel graveyard restored and landscaped.
1981-1982	19th century chapel gutted and completely renovated.
1982-1983	New toilet block and kitchen enlarged.
1983	First phase of chapel bungalows completed.
1985-1986	Park hall acquired, dismantled, transported and erected.
1986	New car park and drive resurfaced.
1986-1987	Office block, lounge and schoolrooms erected.
1988	Bungalow project completed.
1989	'Hillview' purchased.
1990	Car park enlarged.
1996	'Hillview' renovated and enlarged.
2000	Haven family centre opened.
2001	New kitchen and main hall enlarged.

MINISTERS OF THE CHURCH

Rev John Hall 1831–1881

Rev Edward Ashton 1881–1899

Rev Henry K Cross 1899–1909

Rev Stanley Cox 1909–1926

Rev L G Schofield 1927–1930

Rev Havelock Roderick 1931–1953

Rev L G Stapleton 1954–1960

Rev Mervyn Evans 1961–1974

Rev Patrick J Goodland MBE 1976–1994

Rev John Lewis 1996–